Adventures Through World History!
Activities to Engage ALL Students

Rickey Millwood

© 2008 **Kagan Publishing**

This book is published by **Kagan Publishing**. All rights are reserved by **Kagan Publishing**. No part of this publication may be reproduced or transmitted in any form by any means, electronic or mechanical, including photocopy, recording, or any information storage and retrieval system, without prior written permission from **Kagan Publishing**. The blackline masters may be duplicated only by classroom teachers who purchase the book and only for use in their own classrooms. To obtain additional copies of this book, other **Kagan** publications or information regarding professional development, contact **Kagan**.

Kagan Publishing
981 Calle Amanecer
San Clemente, CA 92673
1 (800) 933-2667
Fax: (949) 369-6311
www.KaganOnline.com

ISBN: 978-1-879097-97-1

Introduction

by Rickey Millwood

After teaching American and World History for 26 years and currently serving as the South Carolina Reading Initiative Literacy Coach at Spartanburg High School, I am truly enjoying my educational career more then ever. The students in my classroom are learning more and continue to perform better because their various learning styles are being addressed daily. The reason: I am now teaching with the Kagan structures and activities, which address all learners. I am able to meet the state standards and meet the needs of all my students, not just a select few.

I have been a longtime proponent of active learning in the classroom. I believe students learn best through activities that address all learning styles. I have attended many workshops over the years and have conducted workshops for the South Carolina State Department of Education on active learning in the classroom. However, in all my years of teaching, nothing has made a greater impact on my instruction than the implementation of multiple intelligence strategies I learned by attending a summer Kagan workshop.

After the workshop, I began to develop history activities to engage students' eight intelligences:
- Verbal/Linguistic
- Logical/Mathematical
- Visual/Spatial
- Musical/Rhythmic
- Bodily/Kinesthetic
- Naturalist
- Interpersonal
- Intrapersonal

I broadened my activities and had my students make posters, draw political cartoons, sing songs, conduct research, create graphs, and role-play events. Immediately, I enjoyed tremendous success. World History became more active and real for my classes. Engaging students in meaningful activities greatly enhances student performance and motivation.

Discipline problems virtually disappeared. Many teachers recognize that discipline is a major issue in schools across the nation. However, when a teacher is able to tap into the learning style of all students, students stay on task and are involved in the learning process. Your discipline will improve because the learning is centered around the student. By adding the Kagan strategies to my teaching style, I witnessed so many positive changes.

By engaging all students in a variety of activities that span the intelligences, all learning styles are met on a daily basis. The students—not the teacher—are at the center of the learning. Students experience world history from the inside, rather than merely hearing a lecture.

There are 20 chapters in this book and 100 blackline masters. These masters contain a lead-in summary that brings in the literacy element. The final chapter titled "The Modern World" contains 20 masters on recent events around the globe. To do each activity would be impossible. Simply decide which activities you feel would be best suited for your students. For instance, you may address three learning styles per day, and then select another three the following day. Just continue to rotate through all the learning styles in each unit. The masters rotate through the intelligences from unit to unit as well. The masters focus upon political, social, economic, and environmental issues. Some masters contain problem-solving activities and engagements that require the use of computer technology.

The state standards provide the teacher with information the students should learn. The standards tell us what the students should be able to do at the completion of each unit. This activity book will assist you in taking all of your students to the destination of the standard. You will not only meet the standard, but you will also meet the needs of the diverse learner. Truly, no learning style will be left behind. You will move the entire class to the desired goals. You will see better grades, a better quality of work, and most importantly, you will see students desiring to come to your class. I have personally experienced many students telling me that they love the World History course because it came alive for them. I have experienced students stopping before they leave class to say thanks for preparing the activities. This is truly a most rewarding experience. I feel that I have been able to change so many young minds and attitudes toward this subject. Now, I am sharing these activities with you through this book.

Use these Kagan MI activities daily in you lessons and you will see your students perform better than ever. Just watch their grades and attitudes improve. Not only will you be teaching your favorite content, you will be building the skills that our students so desperately need after graduation. Your lessons will also allow the students to become better readers and writers because you are bringing in a literacy element. Most of all, you will enjoy your teaching more and your students will fall in love with world history. I am confident you will find many activities to engage your students while you meet the various standards.

Acknowledgements
- Miguel Kagan—Concept and Development
- Erin Kant—Illustration
- Jennifer Duke—Graphic Design
- Becky Herrington—Publications Manager
- Alex Core—Cover Layout and Color
- Kimberly Fields—Copyediting

World History Standards Through Multiple Intelligence Activities

It has been my experience as a classroom teacher that all state standards can be met while addressing diverse learners. Our state standards spell out to us what our students are to learn, so we must devise our own road map to that destination. By recognizing that all students learn differently, we have taken the first step toward meeting the needs of our students. Instruction through the use of multiple intelligence activities on a daily basis moves the entire class toward the goal of the standard. We accommodate all learners when we take into account that our classrooms are full of diverse students. By actively engaging students, you will not only meet the standard, you will also move all of your students—not just a select few—toward that goal. Your students will become motivated and enjoy attending your class. I have witnessed students working harder and have seen their grades improve. Most importantly, you will see an attitude change in your students. The quality of their work will improve because they will appreciate what you are doing to help them learn.

Global Studies Standards Addressed in this Workbook

- ○ The Ancient Civilizations
- ○ The Classical Civilizations
- ○ The Dark and Middle Ages
- ○ The African Kingdoms
- ○ Exploration and Discovery
- ○ The Advanced Indian Civilizations
- ○ The Renaissance and the Reformation
- ○ Scientific Reasoning and the Enlightenment
- ○ Democratic Revolution and Industrial Growth
- ○ The World Wars
- ○ The Holocaust
- ○ Era of the Cold War
- ○ The Middle East
- ○ Current World Issues

Table of Contents

Chapter 1—Ancient Egypt (4000 BC–1000 BC) 6

Chapter 2—Ancient Greece (2500 BC–100 BC) 14

Chapter 3—Ancient Rome (509 BC–AD 476) 22

Chapter 4—The Dark and Middle Ages (500–1500) 30

Chapter 5—The Kingdoms of Ghana, Mali, and Songhai (500–1591) 38

Chapter 6—The Renaissance and the Reformation (1300–1600) 46

Chapter 7—The Age of Discovery (1450–1750) 54

Chapter 8—The Advanced Civilizations of Mexico and Peru (500–1550) 62

Chapter 9—The Scientific Revolution and the Enlightenment (1550–1789) 70

Chapter 10—The Age of Democratic Revolution (1640–1830) 78

Chapter 11—The Industrial Revolution (1700–1900) 86

Chapter 12—Era of World War I (1914–1920) 94

Chapter 13—The Rise of Dictators (1919–1939) 102

Chapter 14—The Holocaust (1933–1945) 110

Chapter 15—World War II (1939–1945) 118

Chapter 16—The Cold War (1945–1991) 126

Chapter 17—Events in Asia after World War II (1945–1995) 134

Chapter 18—Turmoil in Southeast Asia (1945–2000) 142

Chapter 19—Recent Events in the Middle East (1975–2007) 150

Chapter 20—Recent Events in the Modern World (1980–2007) 158
- Political Events and Issues 162
- Environmental Issues 173
- Social and Economic Issues 178

Chapter 1: Ancient Egypt (4000 BC—1000 BC)

We still marvel at the accomplishments of the ancient Egyptians. We usually think of pharaohs, pyramids, and hidden treasure when Egypt first comes to mind. This civilization was highly advanced and contributed much to modern society.

Located in the northeastern part of Africa, Egypt prospered because of the Nile River. The Nile brought life and prosperity to this arid region in ancient times.

Verbal/Linguistic

1 Read about the unusual features of the Nile River.

2 Read about the Great Pyramids in Egypt.

3 Read about the importance of the pharaoh to Egyptian society.

4 Write a poem about an Egyptian pharaoh.

5 Share ideas about the medical practices of ancient Egypt.

6 Examine pictures of Egyptian art, and then write a story about what is taking place in the picture.

7 Discuss the purpose of the Sphinx.

8 Share thoughts about the discovery of King Tutankhamen.

9 Write a biography of Howard Carter, the archaeologist that discovered King Tut's burial chamber.

10 Compare and contrast the discovery of Howard Carter to that of Heinrich Schliemann.

Logical/Mathematical

1 Analyze data about the building of the Egyptian pyramids.

2 Sequence the events or steps in building a pyramid.

3 Brainstorm ideas that explain how the Egyptians lifted an obelisk.

4 Calculate the weight and height of an obelisk.

5 Determine the distance that the Nile covers when it overflows its banks.

6 Determine the distance that the Nile flows through Egypt.

7 Estimate the value of the treasure from King Tut's tomb.

8 Sequence the steps in mummification.

9 Synthesize ideas about the calendar used by the Egyptians.

10 Compare and contrast the Egyptian and Mayan pyramids.

Adventures Through World History! • Rickey Millwood

Visual/Spatial

1 Create a drawing of the construction of the Great Pyramid.

2 Examine a picture of the Sphinx and express your thoughts on its purpose.

3 Design an Egyptian obelisk.

4 Examine and interpret pictures of Egyptian hieroglyphics.

5 View the artifacts removed from King Tut's tomb.

6 Create a PowerPoint about Egyptian medicine and medical instruments.

7 Chart the flow of the Nile River on a map.

8 Imagine you were a great Egyptian pharaoh designing your burial chamber in a pyramid.

9 Build a model of an Egyptian pyramid.

10 Design a postcard about ancient Egypt.

11 Draw a scene about the Egyptian gods.

12 Examine a picture of the Rosetta Stone.

Musical/Rhythmic

1 Evaluate the purpose of music in Egyptian society.

2 List the musical instruments played by the Egyptians.

3 Learn about the different types of dances performed by Egyptians.

4 Learn about the social classes that were engaged in Egyptian music.

5 Write a song about pyramid building.

6 Write a song about an Egyptian pharaoh.

7 Play an instrument in class that evolved from ancient Egypt.

8 Compare and contrast instruments used in ancient Egypt to modern musical instruments.

9 Create a rap song about Howard Carter.

10 Research the importance of music to the Egyptians engaged in military campaigns.

11 Evaluate how Egyptian music was influenced by religion.

Adventures Through World History! • Rickey Millwood

Chapter 1 continued
Ancient Egypt
(4000 BC—1000 BC)

Bodily/Kinesthetic

1 Build a model of an Egyptian pyramid.

2 Build a model of the Aswan Dam.

3 Build a model of the Rosetta Stone.

4 Build a model of an Egyptian obelisk.

5 Visit a museum that exhibits Egyptian artifacts.

6 Visit museums that host the replicas from King Tut's tomb.

7 Act out the role of an Egyptian that worked on the Great Pyramid.

8 Role-play the Sphinx and describe your purpose and dimensions.

9 Create a class project about the history of the Suez Canal and its economic impact on Egypt.

10 Act out the role of various Egyptian pharaohs and describe your contributions to Egypt.

Naturalist

1 List the features of the Nile River.

2 Explain how mud from the Nile can be used as an antibiotic.

3 Record the changes in the Nile after the construction of the Aswan Dam.

4 Record the importance of silt deposits of the Nile.

5 List the materials used to build the Great Pyramids.

6 List the characteristics of a stone barge that transported stone to the location of the pyramids.

7 Write about the tools used to chisel stone from Egyptian quarries.

8 Classify medical instruments used by Egyptian physicians.

9 Describe how papyrus was used to make paper.

10 List the materials used in mummification.

11 Record the steps in mummification.

12 Observe the intricate gold work in the facial mask placed over King Tut.

Adventures Through World History! • Rickey Millwood
Kagan Publishing • 1 (800) 933-2667 • www.KaganOnline.com

Interpersonal

1 Discuss with a partner how the Great Pyramid was constructed.

2 Practice taking turns stating the importance of the Nile to the Egyptians.

3 Solve problems that architects confronted in building the Aswan Dam.

4 Solve problems architects confronted in building the Suez Canal.

5 Do a team presentation on the religious practices in ancient Egypt.

6 Interview each other about the discovery of King Tut's tomb.

7 Share with others information about King Ramses.

8 Discuss with a partner the medical practices of Egyptian physicians.

9 Reach a consensus on the importance of studying ancient Egypt.

10 Plan a festival around ancient Egypt.

11 Interview a member of the community that has traveled to Egypt.

12 With a classmate, examine pictures inside the Cairo Museum on the Internet.

Intrapersonal

1 Prioritize the materials needed to construct a pyramid.

2 Make an action plan to control the flooding of the Nile.

3 Describe your feelings about the discovery of King Tut's tomb.

4 Create a diary as if you were Howard Carter searching for King Tut.

5 Defend the position by the Egyptian authorities not to allow the artifacts from King Tut's tomb to travel out of Egypt.

6 Write a personal poem about the Egyptian hieroglyphics.

7 Think about the purpose of the Sphinx.

8 Write about the discovery of the Rosetta Stone.

9 Write an ethical code of treatment for those that constructed the pyramids.

10 Express your likes and dislikes about Egyptian medical practices.

11 Describe your feelings about the contributions the ancient Egyptians made in music.

12 Defend or condemn the religious views of the ancient Egyptians.

13 Write about the importance of Egyptian history.

14 Take a stance to support the importance of the pharaoh to Egyptian culture.

1.1 Blackline Master • Interpersonal Activity

Ancient Egypt

The Pyramids

The pyramids of Egypt are certainly breathtaking. These magnificent structures were created by the pharaohs as an eternal resting chamber. To the Egyptians, the pharaoh was a god to be deified. These pyramids were stocked with all sorts of items that the pharaoh would need in the next life.

The most remarkable find was made by Howard Carter in 1922 when he discovered the tomb of King Tut. It had been undisturbed for centuries. This gives us a glimpse into the importance of the pyramid in Egyptian society.

Instructions: Imagine you were the architect in charge of building the Great Pyramid. Address the following problems you will confront as you construct this massive structure.

Labor force: _____
_____

Transportation of stone: _____
_____

Calculating the dimensions of the pyramid: _____
_____

Temperature in the desert: _____
_____

Lifting and fitting the stone: _____
_____

Designing hidden chambers to conceal the pharaoh: _____
_____

Adventures Through World History! • Rickey Millwood
Kagan Publishing • 1 (800) 933-2667 • www.KaganOnline.com

1.2 Blackline Master • Intrapersonal Activity

Ancient Egypt

Constructing the Pyramids

The labor that went into constructing a pyramid was enormous. Just imagine being a member of a labor gang that worked on these pyramids. Some of these pyramids took 20 years to construct. These pyramids are more than just structures in history; they are powerful symbols that show the supreme building and architectural skills of the Egyptians.

Instructions: Describe your feelings about the Egyptian workers who constructed colossal pyramids.

_____
_____
_____
_____
_____
_____
_____
_____
_____
_____
_____
_____
_____
_____
_____
_____

Adventures Through World History! • Rickey Millwood
Kagan Publishing • 1 (800) 933-2667 • www.KaganOnline.com

1.3 Blackline Master • Naturalist Activity

Ancient Egypt

The Nile River

The Nile is perhaps the most famous river in the world. The Nile is the longest river in the world and flows from south to north. It journeys through Egypt and empties into the Mediterranean Sea.

The feature that makes the Nile different from other rivers is that its flooding is predictable—the Nile floods the same time each year. It deposits rich silt. Egyptians have been able to farm this region for centuries.

The Nile also contains a type of mud that contains an antibiotic. The Egyptians used this in their medical practices. The Nile truly brings life to this arid desert region.

Instructions: Create a list of seven features or characteristics of the Nile River.

1. _____
2. _____
3. _____
4. _____
5. _____
6. _____
7. _____

Adventures Through World History! • Rickey Millwood
Kagan Publishing • 1 (800) 933-2667 • www.KaganOnline.com

1.4 Blackline Master • Visual/Spatial Activity

Ancient Egypt

Tourism in Egypt

Thousands of tourists travel to Egypt each year to tour this magnificent country. One may take a tour to the great Cairo Museum to visit the Great Pyramids. The Egyptian economy counts heavily on tourism from America, and the threat of terrorism and violence in the region affects tourism. Safety is always the main concern to tourists. People are simply afraid to vacation in this region because of violence. The recent violence in the summer of 2006 between Israel and Hezbollah frightens tourists away. Americans are staying in the United States to vacation. Therefore, the economies of Egypt and the nations in the Middle East region suffer because of violence and terrorism.

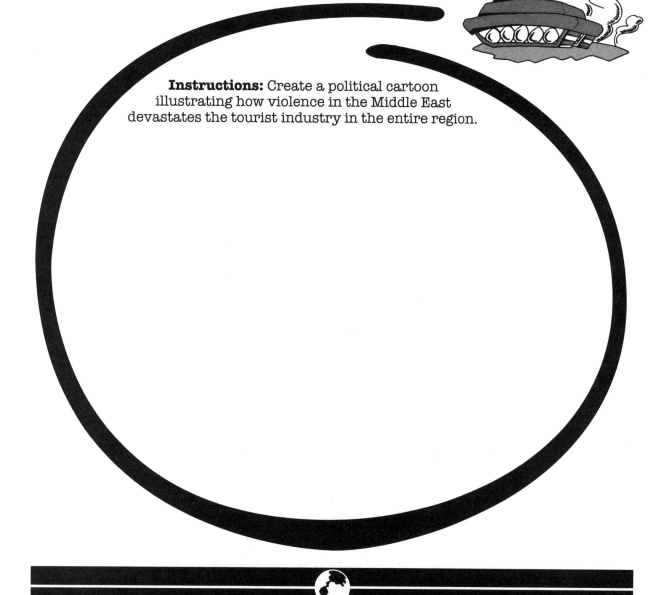

Instructions: Create a political cartoon illustrating how violence in the Middle East devastates the tourist industry in the entire region.

Adventures Through World History! • Rickey Millwood
Kagan Publishing • 1 (800) 933-2667 • www.KaganOnline.com

Chapter 2

Ancient Greece
(2500 BC–100 BC)

The ancient Greeks made tremendous contributions to the modern world. Many of these gifts influence our daily lives. These remarkable people created magnificent works in the fields of architecture, literature, philosophy, and sports. Travelers to Greece today stand in awe when gazing upon the Parthenon and Theater of Epidaurus. Religion dominated the culture of ancient Greece and influenced all aspects of life. Stories about Greek gods and goddesses give us a glimpse into a time when the Greeks dominated the Aegean world.

Verbal/Linguistic

1 Conduct read-alouds from *The Iliad* and *The Odyssey*.

2 Discuss the Trojan War around 1200 BC.

3 Discuss the possibility that the Greeks gave a wooden horse to Troy.

4 Write a poem about Helen of Troy.

5 Write a newspaper article about the fall of Troy.

6 Do a descriptive writing exercise about one of the Greek gods or goddesses.

7 Compare and contrast the ancient Olympics with the modern Olympics.

8 Write a book report on a Greek playwright.

9 Do a creative writing exercise on life in ancient Sparta.

10 Write a narrative about the 300 Spartans at Thermopylae.

11 Write a speech advocating the construction of the Parthenon after the Persian Wars.

12 Write a play that could have been performed in ancient Greece.

Logical/Mathematical

1 List and organize facts about Pythagoras.

2 Determine how the theories of Euclid have a place in modern architecture.

3 Chart the route from Marathon to Athens that Pheidippides ran bringing the news of a Greek victory.

4 Sequence the events that led to the invasion of Greece by King Xerxes of Persia.

5 Make predictions about the outcome at the battle of Thermopylae, based on data.

6 Compare Greek medicine and healing with modern science.

7 Sequence the events that led to the building of the Parthenon.

8 Examine potential problems with the construction of the Theater of Epidaurus.

9 Make associations between democracy in Athens and American democracy.

10 Create a graphic organizer about the conquests of Alexander the Great.

11 Examine the Greek alphabet and synthesize ideas about its creation.

Visual/Spatial

1 Watch the film *Troy*.

2 Watch the film *The Odyssey*.

3 Watch the film *Three Hundred*.

4 Draw a scene from everyday life in ancient Greece.

5 Build a model of the Parthenon.

6 Chart the route covered by Xerxes as he invaded Greece.

7 Create a political cartoon about the trial of Socrates.

8 Create a postage stamp of the Wooden Horse of Troy.

9 Draw a scene depicting the fall of Troy.

10 Paint or draw a picture of Helen of Troy.

11 Create a model of *Winged Victory*.

12 Make a poster about Spartan women.

13 Design a brochure about travel in ancient Greece.

14 Create an illustration about the ancient Olympics.

15 Watch the film *Alexander*.

Musical/Rhythmic

1 Identify the musical instruments played in ancient Greece.

2 Perform in front of the class an instrument played in ancient Greece.

3 Determine patterns in the music of ancient Greece.

4 Relate Greek music to warfare.

5 Evaluate the music performed in Greek theaters.

6 Write a song about a major event from ancient Greece.

7 Create a song about a Greek hero.

8 Compose a melody about an ancient Olympic event.

9 Create a rap song about the Wooden Horse of Troy.

10 Find any patterns in the design of Greek musical instruments.

11 Sing a song in class about a Greek god or goddess.

12 Learn about Pan, the Greek god of music.

Adventures Through World History! • Rickey Millwood

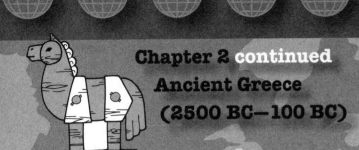

Chapter 2 continued
Ancient Greece
(2500 BC—100 BC)

Bodily/Kinesthetic

1. Act out the role of a Greek warrior about to climb inside the Trojan horse.
2. Perform a skit about Helen of Troy.
3. Build a model of the Parthenon.
4. Visit Greece on the Internet and make a presentation to the class.
5. Visit the Parthenon in Nashville, Tennessee.
6. Visit any buildings illustrating Greek architecture.
7. Perform a skit about the trial of Socrates.
8. Act out the role of citizens in ancient Greece discussing democracy.
9. Perform a skit about the 300 Spartans at Thermopylae.
10. Perform a dance from ancient Greece.
11. Role-play spectators in a Greek theater discussing the works of Euripides.
12. Re-create an ancient Olympic event.
13. Build a wreath of leaves presented to the winner of a Greek sporting event.
14. Re-create an experiment conducted by Archimedes.

Naturalist

1. Create a display of foods eaten by the ancient Greeks.
2. Observe the Parthenon via the Internet.
3. Examine the planets and constellations named by the Greeks.
4. List the characteristics of the topography of Greece.
5. Examine photographs on the Internet of the treasure of Troy discovered by Heinrich Schliemann.
6. Research the importance that marble quarries played in Greek architecture.
7. Record the stages in the construction of the Parthenon.
8. Determine the materials used to construct the Colossus of Rhodes.
9. List the characteristics of the Aegean Sea.
10. Create a PowerPoint about the physical features of Greece.
11. Report on relics from Crete.
12. Learn about the varieties of grapes grown in Greece.
13. Create a chart of natural plants used in Greek medicine.
14. Categorize the major agricultural or mineral exports from Greece.

Adventures Through World History! • Rickey Millwood
Kagan Publishing • 1 (800) 933-2667 • www.KaganOnline.com

Interpersonal

1 Do a team presentation about Greek mythology.

2 Mediate an end to the Peloponnesian War.

3 Discuss with a partner the conquests of Alexander the Great.

4 Solve problems that the Greeks would have faced in constructing the Parthenon.

5 Discuss with a partner the political views of Aristotle.

6 Interview other classmates about a famous Greek playwright.

7 Practice active listening as classmates point out the major accomplishments from classical Greece.

8 Practice taking turns discussing movies made about Greek heroes.

9 Plan to watch the movie *Clash of the Titans*.

10 Share with others the importance that sports played in ancient Greece.

11 Write a collaborative paper on movies or films made about ancient Greek heroes.

12 Critique, as a class, a film about a Greek hero.

Intrapersonal

1 Think about the actions of Socrates at the conclusion of his trial.

2 Describe your feelings about ancient Sparta.

3 Make a journal entry as if you were a soldier serving Alexander the Great.

4 Express your likes and dislikes about the ancient Olympic games.

5 Relate ancient Greek architecture with modern architecture.

6 Think about the actions of the Greek physician Hippocrates and the art of healing.

7 Choose between the alternatives to defend the passage at Thermopylae by the Greeks or surrender to the Persians.

8 Take a stance in ancient Greece to allow women to participate in the democratic process.

9 Write an ethical code for women's rights in ancient Greece.

10 Write an ethical code of conduct toward the Helots in ancient Sparta.

11 Write about the needs of an ancient Greek astronomer.

12 Write about your views on the theory that a wooden horse was given to Troy.

13 Write about the influence that ancient Greece has had on the modern world.

14 Write a personal poem about a major event in ancient Greece.

15 Relate any content from the study of ancient Greece to a personal experience.

Ancient Greece

The Ancient Olympic Games

The ancient Olympics began in 776 BC. These games were to honor the gods of Greece, but they were also intended to keep men in shape for military duty. The games were held every four years—usually in late August or early September. Events in the games included running, throwing, wrestling, and jumping events.

The modern Olympics began in 1896 in Athens, Greece. Nations and athletes from all over the world compete for medals and prestige.

The ancient Greeks intended the games to be played for entirely different purposes than they are played today. Yet, some similarities do exist. In recent history, tragic events have marred the Olympics and often nations have boycotted the games for political reasons.

Instructions: Research, and present in groups, the political drama that surrounded the following summer Olympics.

(1936) (1972) (1980) (1984)

Ancient Greece

A Brave Stand at Thermopylae

Two powerful Persian kings plagued the Greeks with invading armies around 490 BC. The first Persian king who tried to conquer Greece was Darius I, but the Greeks defeated him at Marathon. Xerxes I, the son of Darius, vowed revenge and tried to finish the job his father had started. Some estimate that the army of Xerxes numbered close to 500,000. This may be an exaggeration; nevertheless it was an enormous invading force.

The Greeks tried to stop Xerxes in a narrow passage in northern Greece called Thermopylae. Three hundred brave Spartans blocked the passage for several days. However, they were eventually betrayed, and the Persians fought their way into Greece. The Persians destroyed Athens, but the Greeks rallied. The Greeks finally drove Xerxes from their soil. A united Greece had defeated this foreign invader.

Instructions: Make a journal entry from the point of view of a Persian soldier after seeing 300 Spartans block the passage at Thermopylae.

Ancient Greece

Constructing the Parthenon

Perhaps the most famous of all Greek structure ever constructed is the Parthenon. Over 2,000 years old, the Parthenon gives us a glimpse of the beauty of ancient Greece. This structure, created after the Persian Wars, demonstrates the advancement of ancient Greek mathematics and architecture.

No expense was spared to create this magnificent temple. This structure was more than a building to honor Athena—it represents the glory of Greece. Tourists continue to flock to Greece to see one of the most famous structures in the world.

Instructions: In teams, form solutions to the problems the Greeks would have faced in constructing the Parthenon. Consider the following: obtaining materials, skilled labor, engineering challenges, and mathematical computations.

2.4 Blackline Master • Bodily/Kinesthetic Activity

Ancient Greece

A Night at the Theater

Imagine a time in the past in which one could attend the Greek theater and see the plays of Sophocles, Aristophanes, Euripides, and Aeschylus. Just as the Greeks had constructed temples, such as the Parthenon, they also constructed outdoor theaters.

The theater of Epidaurus is an outdoor Greek theater built into the side of a hill. It seats nearly 14,000 and has perfect acoustics. One can be seated on the back row and hear a whisper from the stage! These theaters were the home for comedies and tragedies performed before thousands of spectators. Some of these plays have actually survived centuries of time and are still performed today.

Instructions: Select a famous Greek playwright. Write a monologue discussing the playwright's life or one of his plays. Perform your monologue for a partner or the class.

_____
_____
_____
_____
_____
_____
_____
_____
_____
_____
_____
_____
_____

Adventures Through World History! • Rickey Millwood
Kagan Publishing • 1 (800) 933-2667 • www.KaganOnline.com

Chapter 3

Ancient Rome
(509 BC–AD 476)

One of the greatest civilizations was the mighty Roman Empire. The empire emerged on the Tiber River in Italy. Rome expanded and conquered several million square miles of territory. At the height of the empire, Rome ruled over nearly seventy million people.

The great empire was held together by the strength of its powerful army and Roman law. The Roman Republic and Roman Empire lasted nearly a thousand years. Today, the legacy of Rome is found throughout the world.

Verbal/Linguistic

1 Analyze the phrase, "All roads lead to Rome."

2 Compare and contrast the Greek and Roman armies.

3 Do a creative writing exercise about an event in the Roman Colosseum.

4 Write a persuasive paper arguing for the abolition of gladiatorial games.

5 Do a creative writing exercise on the revolt of Spartacus.

6 Create a speech about the opening of the Circus Maximus.

7 Write a poem about a famous Roman chariot driver.

8 Write a eulogy for Julius Caesar.

9 Create a slogan about the Roman legions.

10 Debate the use of wild animals in the Roman Colosseum.

11 Write a speech by Nero concerning the Great Fire of Rome.

12 Explain the concept of the Pax Romana.

Logical/Mathematical

1 Evaluate the impact that Rome had upon the modern world.

2 Form a plan that architects would have used to construct a top on the Roman Colosseum.

3 Analyze data about the Roman legions.

4 Brainstorm ideas about the impact of Roman roads.

5 Sequence the events that led to the death of Julius Caesar.

6 Discover trends in the Roman policy of persecution toward the Christians.

7 List the causes of the fall of the Roman Empire.

8 Synthesize ideas that could have possibly saved Rome from decay.

9 Sequence the major events that led to the fall of Rome.

10 List and organize facts about the last Roman emperors.

11 Make associations between the fall of Rome and economic problems in America.

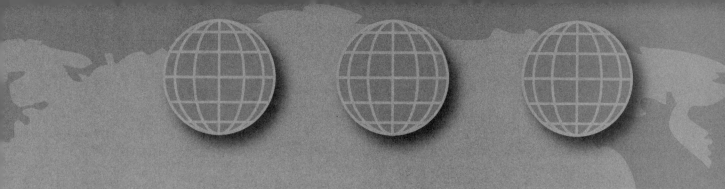

Visual/Spatial

1 Watch the film *Spartacus*.

2 Watch the film *Gladiator*.

3 Watch the film *Quo Vadis*.

4 Watch the film *Ben-Hur*.

5 Draw a scene about the games held in the Colosseum.

6 Create a flyer advertising a chariot race in the Circus Maximus.

7 Imagine you were trained to be a gladiator and forced to compete in the Colosseum.

8 Build a model of the Roman Colosseum.

9 Design a postcard about the glory of ancient Rome.

10 Draw a map of the Roman Empire and label the major regions.

11 Draw a scene about the Great Fire of Rome.

12 Create a political cartoon about Nero and the Great Fire of Rome.

13 Create a PowerPoint about Roman medicine.

14 Design a book cover about the mighty Roman Empire.

Musical/Rhythmic

1 Write a song about a major event in the history of Rome.

2 Evaluate the music played at Roman sporting events.

3 Learn about the major instruments played by the Romans.

4 Conduct research on the story of Nero playing on a fiddle as Rome burned.

5 Compose a melody about Julius Caesar.

6 Compare and contrast Greek and Roman musical instruments.

7 Write a report about the use of instruments during Roman battles.

8 List the musical instruments invented by the Romans.

9 Write a jingle about the Roman legions.

10 Create a rap song about the elements that caused the fall of the Roman Empire.

Chapter 3 continued
Ancient Rome
(509 BC—AD 476)

Bodily/Kinesthetic

1. Build a model of the Roman Colosseum, Circus Maximus, or Pantheon.
2. Role-play an engineer planning the building of the Colosseum.
3. Visit ancient Rome on the Internet and share the experience with the class.
4. Perform a skit about the role of women in the Roman world.
5. Act out the role of Spartacus speaking against the Roman policy of slavery.
6. Act out the role of Roman citizens in the final days of the empire.
7. Act out the role of an emperor trying to hold the Roman Empire together.
8. Perform a skit about a famous Roman chariot driver.
9. Build a model of the city of Rome.
10. Build a model of a Roman aqueduct.
11. Act out the role of a Roman soldier that served in the legions for 20 years.
12. Use physical gestures to show a Roman's emotions at the Colosseum.
13. Build a model of a Roman ship.
14. Perform a pantomime about a major event in the history of Rome.

Naturalist

1. List the characteristics of the climate in Italy.
2. Examine on the Internet pictures of Roman aqueducts and the terrain they crossed.
3. Examine pictures of the Alps, which were crossed by Hannibal with elephants.
4. Classify the materials used to construct Roman roads.
5. Observe the materials used to build Roman helmets.
6. Classify the natural materials found to design a Roman military uniform.
7. Observe the structure and materials used to construct the Pantheon.
8. Create a display of the major foods consumed by the Romans.
9. Record the changes in Pompeii after the eruption of Mt. Vesuvius.
10. Classify the names of the Roman planets.
11. Record the changes in Rome after the great fire in AD 64.
12. Observe pictures of the animals used in Roman sports.

Interpersonal

1 Share opinions with classmates about life in the Roman Republic and the Roman Empire.

2 Discuss with a partner the problems that brought down the mighty Roman Empire.

3 Interview other classmates about great Roman building projects.

4 Debate the issue of gladiatorial fighting.

5 Reach a consensus explaining why Jerusalem was destroyed in AD 70.

6 Discuss the actions of Pontius Pilate as Governor of Palestine.

7 Discuss with a classmate the repercussions from the Great Fire of Rome.

8 Do a team presentation on Roman law.

9 Mediate the conflict between Hannibal and the Romans.

10 Share with others the importance of the Roman legions.

11 Discuss with a classmate women's rights in the Roman Empire.

Intrapersonal

1 Describe your feelings about individuals who were forced to become gladiators.

2 Observe the mood changes in Rome after Julius Caesar destroyed the Roman Republic.

3 Think about the actions of a soothsayer warning Caesar to beware of the Ides of March.

4 Express your likes and dislikes about Julius Caesar.

5 List the priorities of Nero after the Great Fire of Rome.

6 Write about the actions of the barbarians that destroyed Rome.

7 Write an ethical code of the humane treatment of prisoners captured by the Romans.

8 Defend the position by Constantine to split the Roman Empire.

9 Describe your feelings about Roman architects and engineers.

10 Write a personal poem about the fall of the Roman Empire.

Ancient Rome

Roman Sports and Recreation

The Romans craved violent sports. The Colosseum, the world's most recognizable stadium, was the sight of bloody gladiatorial games for centuries. The Colosseum was more than a sports arena; it symbolized the grandeur of Rome. The Circus Maximus, a enormous race track, was home to the major chariot races in Rome. Charioteers gave the audience quite a thrill in action-packed races.

The games were held more than just for the sake of sports. These games were tied in with social control and religion. The emperors gave the people what they wanted to see daily. Romans craved brutality, and the fans were able to participate by deciding life and death. Gladiators died by the thousands as the spectators cheered wildly for their favorites.

Instructions: Imagine you were a Roman citizen and regularly attended the events in the Colosseum or Circus Maximus. Write a letter to a friend describing the feeling of being in these stadiums as the events unfolded.

Ancient Rome

Roman Engineers and Architects

Roman architects were magnificent builders. The architects had a tremendous knowledge of mathematical information to create these structures, and they were able to use concrete in their projects.

The Romans built stadiums, roads, lakes, temples, and aqueducts. Their projects differed from the Greeks in beauty as these were practical and useful projects. These structures define Rome from other civilizations. They were more than just structures; they symbolized the power and glory of the Roman Empire.

Instructions: Place students on teams. Each team selects one of the architectural structures listed below. The team researches and constructs a model of that structure.

- Circus Maximus
- Roman Colosseum
- Pantheon
- Trajan's Column
- Tropaeum Traiani

- Bridge
- Aqueduct
- Forum
- Domus Aurea
- Roman road

3.3 Blackline Master • Verbal/Linguistic Activity

Ancient Rome

The Death of a Dictator

Julius Caesar gained fame in his military campaign against the Gauls in the Gallic Wars. Caesar conquered the Gauls and was prepared to return to Rome. The Senate ordered him to return to Rome without his army. He disobeyed the Senate and crossed the Rubicon River. A period of bitter civil war erupted.

Eventually, Caesar defeated his opponents and came to power. He destroyed the Roman Republic by forcing the Senate to name him dictator. He was killed because he had become an absolute dictator over Rome. The Senate had lost their power to one man.

The most famous of all Romans was butchered by Roman senators. Caesar had destroyed the Roman Republic, now Rome would be an empire, ruled by an emperor. Augustus would become Rome's first emperor.

EXTRA

Instructions: Create a newspaper headline about the death of Julius Caesar. Then, write a major news story about the event and include interviews with those who witnessed his death.

Headline: _____

Adventures Through World History! • Rickey Millwood
Kagan Publishing • 1 (800) 933-2667 • www.KaganOnline.com

3.4 Blackline Master • Interpersonal Activity

Ancient Rome

The Collapse of the Mighty Roman Empire

In AD 476, the Roman Empire came to an end. The last Roman emperor was replaced by a barbarian king. Rome had lasted over a thousand years. Why had the empire crumbled? An analysis shows that Rome suffered from political, economic, and social problems. These factors were interwoven and eventually caused the empire to crumble into decay. Rome has a warning to other civilizations: examine the decay and perhaps avoid the same mistakes that doomed the once mighty empire.

Instructions: Students are placed on teams. Each team researches and reports to the class on one of the following problems the Romans faced in the last years of the empire:

Problem	Team
Barbarian Invasions	
Crime	
Famine and Disease	
Incompetent Rulers	
Military Breakdown	
Moral Decay	
Unemployment	

Adventures Through World History! • Rickey Millwood
Kagan Publishing • 1 (800) 933-2667 • www.KaganOnline.com

Chapter 4: The Dark and Middle Ages (500—1500)

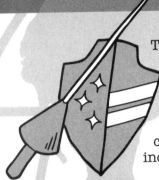

The Dark and Middle Ages reflect a time when mankind faced a lawless situation after the fall of Rome. Barbarians terrified the countryside, and the concept of feudalism emerged to bring some stability back to Europe during this dismal time. This bleak but important time span is the period between the Classical Age and the Renaissance. The Middle Ages was a period of history categorized by several major events upon history's stage. These include the rise of Islam, the Crusades, and the Black Death.

Verbal/Linguistic

1. Read about Mohammed and the founding of Islam.
2. Read about Mohammed's flight to Medina.
3. Discuss life in Europe after the fall of the Roman Empire.
4. Read about the Vikings, and write a report about one aspect of their culture.
5. Write an essay about the causes of the Crusades.
6. Compare and contrast any two medieval kings.
7. Write a poem about a major event in the Middle Ages.
8. Do a descriptive writing exercise about life in a medieval castle.
9. Explain the concept of feudalism.
10. Read about the legend of Robin Hood.
11. Read *The Canterbury Tales*.
12. Write a research paper about medieval punishment and justice.
13. Write about the impact of the Black Death across Europe.

Logical/Mathematical

1. List and organize facts about castle building.
2. Calculate the distance a trebuchet could hurl a boulder or an English longbow could launch an arrow.
3. Make predictions about the elements that brought castle building to an end.
4. Sequence the major events of the Middle Ages.
5. Brainstorm ideas about the failure of the Crusades.
6. Discover patterns in the agricultural practices in the Middle Ages.
7. Classify and categorize medieval weapons.
8. Synthesize ideas about the effects of the Black Death.
9. Calculate the probability of surviving the Black Death in 1348.
10. List and organize facts about the role of women in the Middle Ages.
11. Compare and contrast the Vikings and Huns.

Adventures Through World History! • Rickey Millwood

Visual/Spatial

1 Watch the film *The Vikings*.

2 Watch the film *El Cid*.

3 Watch any films on the Black Death.

4 Watch the film *Joan of Arc*.

5 Create a political cartoon about the Crusades.

6 Estimate the distance the Crusaders covered going to Jerusalem.

7 Chart the routes of the Crusades.

8 Draw a scene about the famine across Europe in 1330.

9 Design a suit of armor a knight could wear to protect himself from arrows.

10 Draw a scene about the Black Death.

11 Examine artwork depicting the plague, and discuss how the plague changed art scenes during the Middle Ages.

12 Imagine you lived in Italy in 1347 when the plague ravaged the country.

13 Design a flier about the Black Death.

14 Create a PowerPoint presentation about medieval siege weapons.

15 Design a book cover about life during the Middle Ages.

Musical/Rhythmic

1 Evaluate the music of medieval ballads.

2 Listen to a song about Robin Hood.

3 Write a rap song about the Crusades.

4 Write a rap song about the Black Death.

5 Research the musical instruments played during the Middle Ages.

6 Sing a song performed by a troubadour of the medieval period.

7 Listen to and determine how music drastically changed during the outbreak of the plague.

8 Compose a melody about a major medieval character.

9 Create a song about the teachings of Mohammed.

10 Determine how historical events affected the music of the Middle Ages.

11 Create a song of courtly love as if written in the Middle Ages.

12 Write a song as if you were a Crusader on the way to Jerusalem.

Adventures Through World History! • Rickey Millwood
Kagan Publishing • 1 (800) 933-2667 • www.KaganOnline.com

Chapter 4 continued
The Dark and Middle Ages (500–1500)

Bodily/Kinesthetic

1 Perform a skit about life on a medieval manor.

2 Visit a Medieval Times dinner theater.

3 Visit a European castle on the Internet and report to the class about its construction.

4 Build a model of a castle or cathedral.

5 Role-play a builder of a great medieval cathedral.

6 Act out the role of a Crusader after returning from the Holy Land.

7 Conduct a medieval trial.

8 Build a model of a trebuchet.

9 Create a model of a medieval manor.

10 Perform a skit or play about the Black Death.

11 Play a sport from the Middle Ages.

12 Act out the role of a knight about to joust for the first time.

13 Act out the role of a knight describing his duties and responsibilities to the feudal lord.

14 Act out the role of a medieval peasant describing his feudal responsibilities.

15 Act out the role of a female during the Middle Ages as she describes her lot in life.

Naturalist

1 List the natural materials used to construct medieval castles.

2 Record the changes in castle building from 1000–1500.

3 Create a display of the foods consumed in the Middle Ages.

4 Categorize the materials used to treat plague victims.

5 Identify the rodent species that carried the Bubonic Plague.

6 List the characteristics of medieval dungeons.

7 Categorize the major physical features of a manor.

8 Categorize materials used by knights to defend themselves.

9 Observe, through pictures or paintings, medieval siege weapons.

10 Classify materials used for clothing in the Middle Ages.

11 Record the changes in agricultural practices due to the three-field system.

12 Record the medieval belief about comets.

Adventures Through World History! • Rickey Millwood
Kagan Publishing • 1 (800) 933-2667 • www.KaganOnline.com

Interpersonal

1 Debate the concept of feudalism.

2 Share with others your thoughts on life in the Middle Ages.

3 Plan a class event about the Middle Ages.

4 Reach a consensus on why the Crusades took place.

5 Discuss with a partner the differences between Roman and medieval justice.

6 Solve problems that medieval towns faced on a daily basis.

7 Discuss with a partner the conquest of England in 1066.

8 Role-play a character of the Middle Ages before the class.

9 Write a collaborative paper on clothing styles in the Middle Ages.

10 Interview each other about the purpose of medieval castles.

11 Assign roles as medieval characters, and discuss methods to combat the outbreak of the Black Death.

12 Reach a consensus explaining why medieval physicians were baffled by the plague.

Intrapersonal

1 Express your likes and dislikes about the concept of feudalism.

2 Create a knight's code of behavior known as *chivalry*.

3 Make an action plan for defending a castle.

4 Describe your feelings about the treatment of women in the Middle Ages.

5 Observe mood changes in Europeans at the conclusion of the Crusades.

6 Think about the actions of the Pope during the Black Death epidemic in 1348.

7 Think about the actions of the flagellants during the plague.

8 Write about the needs of medieval peasants and serfs.

9 Create an argument to abolish jousting tournaments.

10 Write a personal poem about life in the Middle Ages.

11 Keep a daily log as if you were in a castle under siege.

12 Prioritize the military equipment needed by a knight.

4.1 Blackline Master • Bodily/Kinesthetic Activity

The Dark and Middle Ages

The Crusades

The Crusades provided a dramatic moment in history that will forever be remembered. These Crusades—or religious wars—were called for by Pope Urban II to liberate the Holy Land of Jerusalem from the infidels. A religious zeal grabbed Europe for two centuries before the Crusades were completed. This religious fervor swept over Europe; people from all classes went on the Crusades in hope of salvation and riches.

Imagine if you could listen in on a conversation from the past about the Crusades. What would you hear from participants?

Instructions: Place students in five teams. Each team prepares, then performs a brief skit for the class based on the following scenarios:

Team 1—A conversation unfolds between the Pope and his advisors as to why the Crusades are needed

Team 2—A gathering of serfs and peasants discussing why they are going on a Crusade

Team 3—A group of knights describing what they witnessed in Jerusalem on the first Crusade

Team 4—The warriors of Saladin discussing how they plan to drive the Crusaders from the Holy Land

Team 5—Stephen of Cloyes trying to persuade children to join him on a Crusade

Adventures Through World History! • Rickey Millwood
Kagan Publishing • 1 (800) 933-2667 • www.KaganOnline.com

4.2 Blackline Master • Naturalist Activity

The Dark and Middle Ages

Castle Building

Medieval castles come to mind when we think of this period of history. Castles were constructed to offer protection from barbarians after the fall of Rome. Later they were constructed to offer protection from European feudal lords and their armies.

These structures took years to build due to their tremendous size and height. Castle defenders could hold off attackers for months. Sometimes castles were surrounded by a moat to keep enemies away from the walls. These invaders attempted to climb over the walls with tall ladders while intense battles raged.

Attackers also used a variety of siege weapons to gain access to the castles. These included battering rams and trebuchets. Sometimes attackers even tried to dig tunnels under castle walls.

Instructions: Study pictures in books and on the Internet of famous European castles. Then, as a class project, complete the following:

1. Categorize the natural materials used to build castles.

2. Brainstorm and categorize the non-natural items found inside a castle.

3. Record changes in castle construction from 1000–1500.

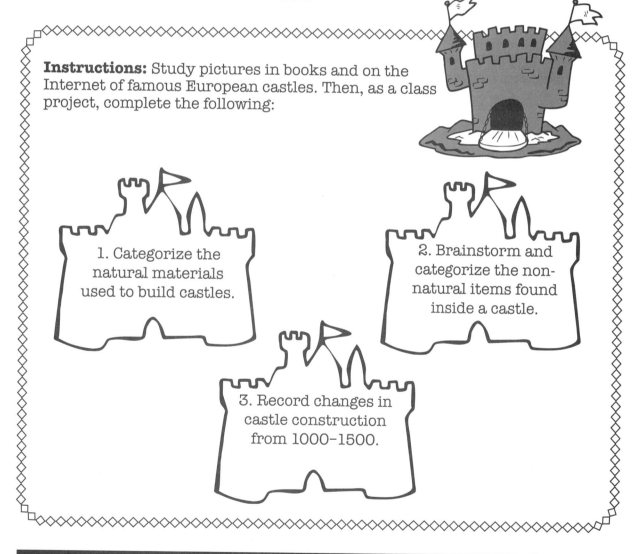

Adventures Through World History! • Rickey Millwood

4.3 Blackline Master • Musical/Rhythmic Activity

The Dark and Middle Ages

The Songs of the Troubadours

Music was important in the Middle Ages. In our minds, we can visualize troubadours singing their songs of courtly love to ladies. The singers often traveled from manor to manor playing their stringed instruments much like our mandolin. These entertainers often performed at medieval fairs, and their songs were often in the form of a story. During the time of the plague, there was a definite break in the music. Music that had once been cheerful suddenly became eerie during this epidemic.

Instructions: Write the lyrics to a song about a major event in the Middle Ages. Then, perform the song and a dance accompanied by musical instruments before the class.

4.4 Blackline Master • Interpersonal Activity

The Dark and Middle Ages

The Black Death

It can be argued that the Black Death, or Bubonic Plague, impacted Europe more than any other event. It affected every single aspect of life across Europe. In fact, Europe lost one-third of its entire population in the 1340s.

This epidemic most likely originated in China and was brought to Italy by merchants that fled Caffa, in the Black Sea region. This disease was highly contagious, and European physicians never determined the cause of the disease nor did they find a cure. The plague totally obliterated European society until around 1352. It is difficult today for us to realize the impact this disease had upon medieval society.

Instructions: In small teams, every student takes the role of one of the following medieval characters. Discuss the causes of the plague and formulate solutions to end this epidemic. Remember to stay true to your role.

- Medieval physician
- Medieval astronomer
- The Pope
- Flagellant
- Medieval peasant
- Medieval feudal lord

Adventures Through World History! • Rickey Millwood
Kagan Publishing • 1 (800) 933-2667 • www.KaganOnline.com

Chapter 5: The African Kingdoms of Ghana, Mali, and Songhai
(500—1591)

The African kingdoms of Ghana, Mali, and Songhai existed from 300 to 1600. These civilizations thrived while Europe suffered through the Middle Ages. The kingdoms prospered due to the organization and trade of salt and gold. These three kingdoms comprised a much larger area than the modern nation states of Ghana and Mali. Mansa Musa, the emperor that brought Islam to Mali, established Timbuktu as a center of learning. Timbuktu became one of the leading cultural centers in the entire world. Following Mali, the empire of Songhai was expanded by Sunni Ali. Islam continued to grow in the region and Islamic laws were enacted. Songhai was conquered by soldiers from Morocco in 1590.

Verbal/Linguistic

1 Discuss the elements that allowed the West African kingdoms to flourish.

2 Compare and contrast the rule of the mansa with the authority of a European feudal lord.

3 Tell a story about an African hero as told by a griot.

4 Do a descriptive writing exercise about Mansa Musa.

5 Learn the vocabulary terms associated with the Sahara Desert.

6 Explain why camels are referred to as the "ship of the desert."

7 Write a research paper on the importance of Timbuktu.

8 Discuss the influence of Islam across North Africa.

9 Write a biography of either Mansa Musa or Sunni Ali.

10 Read about Sundiata and his rule of Songhai.

Logical/Mathematical

1 Analyze data about the importance of the salt trade across Northern Africa.

2 Sequence the events that led to the rise of Ghana, Mali, and Songhai.

3 List and classify items needed to make a long trade journey across the Sahara.

4 Discover patterns that led to strong African mansas.

5 Compare and contrast African and European weapons around the year 1200.

6 Calculate the value of gold per ounce in ancient Mali.

7 Determine the total area in square miles the kingdom of Ghana covered.

8 Calculate the distance from Timbuktu to Cairo.

9 Compare and contrast European and African medicine around the year 1000.

10 Calculate in percentage the number of people in Mali converted to Islam by 1325.

11 Use inductive reasoning to determine how the empire of Songhai became a powerful West African state.

Visual/Spatial

1 Create an illustration that shows the expansion of Ghana, Mali, and Songhai.

2 Chart the route of Mansa Musa across the Sahara Desert to Mecca.

3 Draw a scene from Mansa Musa's crossing of the Sahara.

4 Create an illustration that displays the magnificent city of Timbuktu.

5 Create a postcard about one of the West African kingdoms.

6 Imagine you were a warrior that served with Sunni Ali.

7 Make a poster that illustrates the importance of salt and gold to the West African kingdoms.

8 Create a drawing of a West African home.

9 Examine photographs of clothing worn in the West African kingdoms.

10 Create a PowerPoint about the commerce of Ghana, Mali, and Songhai.

11 Write a story that illustrates how Islam unified the people of the West African kingdom of Mali.

 Musical/Rhythmic

1 Evaluate the importance of music in the West African kingdoms.

2 Listen to current music from West African nations.

3 Compose a melody about Mansa Musa.

4 Learn about the importance of the drum in the West African kingdoms.

5 Learn about the various dances performed in the West African kingdoms.

6 Compare African and European musical instruments from the Middle Ages.

7 Write a song about Mansa Musa's expedition to Mecca.

8 Write a song about a trade item from West Africa.

9 Play as a class musical instruments that come from West Africa.

10 Listen to patterns in music from West Africa and determine their influence on American music.

Adventures Through World History! • Rickey Millwood

Chapter 5 continued
The African Kingdoms of Ghana, Mali, and Songhai (500–1591)

Bodily/Kinesthetic

1 Perform a skit about silent trade.

2 Make a vase like those from West Africa.

3 Design a scene from a West African kingdom.

4 Create a project of the major foods grown in West Africa.

5 Create a display of items from West Africa.

6 Perform a skit about Mansa Musa's journey to Mecca.

7 Dress in clothing in the style West Africans wear today.

8 Perform a dance that originated in West Africa.

9 Do a science experiment that illustrates the importance of salt.

10 Create a crossword puzzle about the kingdoms of West Africa.

11 Act out the role of African women in ancient Mali or Songhai.

12 Create a display of African crafts.

13 Role-play a griot telling a story.

14 Research any sports that originated in West Africa that are popular in America today.

Naturalist

1 List characteristics of the Sahara Desert.

2 Trace the origin and flow of the Niger River.

3 List the characteristics of the savanna.

4 Collect various types of foods consumed by West Africans.

5 Observe at a zoo the animals found in West Africa.

6 Classify the major items used for trade in the West African states.

7 Categorize any plants in America that originated in West Africa.

8 Identify any sections of the United States where crops thrive that originated from West Africa.

9 Record the annual amount of rainfall in a West African nation.

10 Examine a piece of ebony.

11 Classify any natural products used to make medications in West Africa.

12 Conduct research about the importance of Lake Chad and the Niger River.

Adventures Through World History! • Rickey Millwood
Kagan Publishing • 1 (800) 933-2667 • www.KaganOnline.com

Interpersonal

1 Reach a consensus on the importance of salt and gold in Ghana.

2 Practice taking turns giving the importance of the Senegal and Niger Rivers to the Western African kingdoms.

3 With a partner, practice taking turns discussing the importance of Mansa Musa or Sunni Ali.

4 Discuss with a partner how Timbuktu was more advanced than a European city of the same time period.

5 Share with others your thoughts about the significance of Islam to Western Africa.

6 Discuss with a partner the elements that caused the West African kingdoms to thrive.

7 Do a team presentation on the gold artifacts produced by the West African kingdoms.

8 Do a team presentation on the military structure of the West African kingdoms.

9 Share with others the responsibilities of women in the West African kingdoms.

10 Write a collaborative paper on the influence of the African kingdoms to modern West African states.

Intrapersonal

1 Meditate on the importance of the West African kingdoms to the modern world.

2 Weigh alternatives to crossing the Sahara by camel.

3 Describe your feelings about the spread of Islam across Western Africa.

4 Express your likes about the culture of Timbuktu.

5 Write a personal poem about the culture of Ghana, Mali, or Songhai.

6 Describe your feelings about the advancements made in the West African kingdoms.

7 Prioritize the needs of people living in Western Africa today.

8 Choose a modern nation in Western Africa and describe its importance to the rest of the world.

The African Kingdoms of Ghana, Mali, and Songhai

Trade in the West African Kingdoms

The kingdoms of Ghana, Mali, and Songhai stretched across the region we know as Western Africa. These empires were more culturally and economically advanced than Europe at the same time period. These empires were better organized than the feudal kingdoms and manorial states found across medieval Europe. These kingdoms were led and forged by warrior kings such as the famous Mansa Musa of Mali. He is best remembered in history because he brought new ideas from distant places to his kingdom.

Instructions: List the natural materials and foods you feel would be necessary to create a prosperous West African kingdom.

Natural Materials	Foods

The African Kingdoms of Ghana, Mali, and Songhai

Crossing the Sahara

Mansa Musa, the great emperor of Mali, made a pilgrimage across Africa to Mecca. Imagine being one of the party members keeping a journal of the expedition. Remember, you are crossing a vast wilderness of the Sahara Desert where the temperature can climb above 110 degrees each day.

Mansa Musa carried an enormous amount of gold across the region and left no doubt that he was one of the most powerful men in the world. He gathered ideas in the Middle East and brought these back to Mali. His city of Timbuktu was transformed into a magnificent cultural city.

Instructions: Imagine you are Mansa Musa planning your journey across the Sahara. Write about the items you plan to take along and express what you hope to accomplish through this expedition.

5.3 Blackline Master • Logical/Mathematical Activity

The African Kingdoms of Ghana, Mali, and Songhai

Crusade or Pilgrimage?

During the Middle Ages, Europeans made vast treks across Europe on their way to the Holy Land. These Crusades were the most important events of the Middle Ages. About 30 years after the last crusade ended, Mansa Musa made his pilgrimage from Mali to the same region the Crusaders had traveled. In both cases, long distances had been covered and many consequences would result.

Instructions: Compare and contrast the Crusades with the journey made by Mansa Musa to the same region.

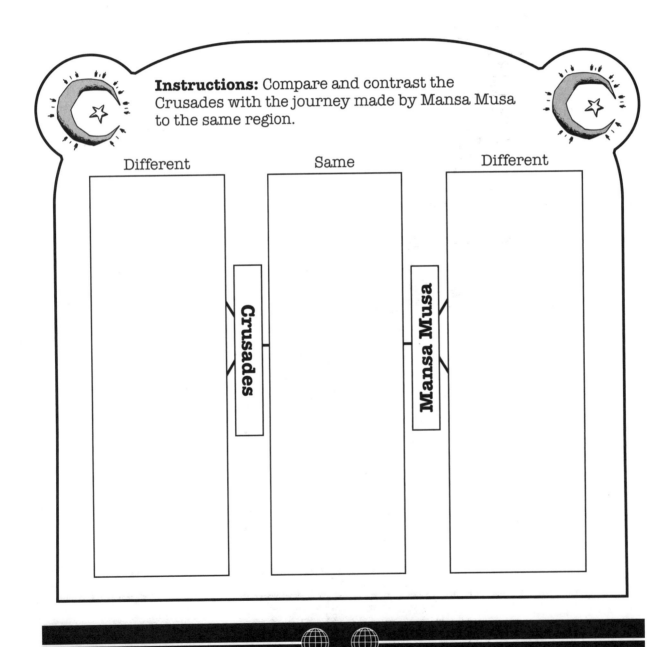

5.4 Blackline Master • Visual/Spatial Activity

The African Kingdoms of Ghana, Mali, and Songhai

The West African Kingdoms

The three kingdoms of Mali, Ghana, and Songhai stretched across the region we know as Western Africa. The empires of Ghana and Mali comprised a region much larger than the modern-day nations. Salt and gold were the two commodities that made these Kingdoms thrive.

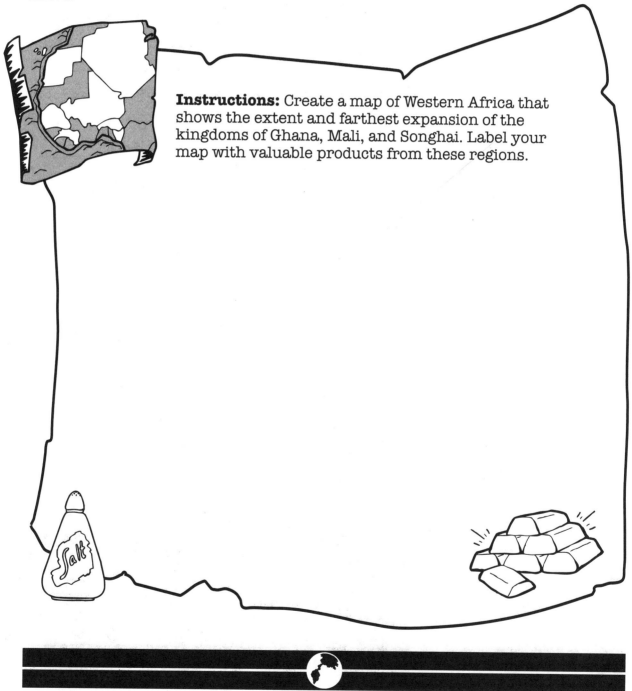

Instructions: Create a map of Western Africa that shows the extent and farthest expansion of the kingdoms of Ghana, Mali, and Songhai. Label your map with valuable products from these regions.

Adventures Through World History! • Rickey Millwood
Kagan Publishing • 1 (800) 933-2667 • www.KaganOnline.com

Chapter 6: The Renaissance and the Reformation (1300–1600)

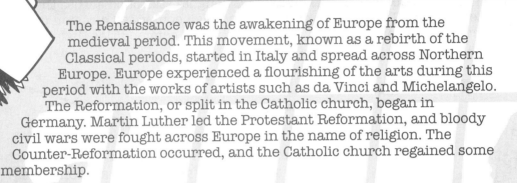

The Renaissance was the awakening of Europe from the medieval period. This movement, known as a rebirth of the Classical periods, started in Italy and spread across Northern Europe. Europe experienced a flourishing of the arts during this period with the works of artists such as da Vinci and Michelangelo. The Reformation, or split in the Catholic church, began in Germany. Martin Luther led the Protestant Reformation, and bloody civil wars were fought across Europe in the name of religion. The Counter-Reformation occurred, and the Catholic church regained some membership.

Verbal/Linguistic

1 Explain the concept of humanism.

2 Discuss the reasons the Renaissance began in Italy.

3 Share ideas explaining why Renaissance artists flocked to Florence, Italy.

4 Write a newspaper article about Lorenzo de Medici.

5 Write a poem about the *Mona Lisa*.

6 Discuss the military drawings of Leonardo da Vinci.

7 Compare and contrast the teachings of John Calvin with the teachings of Martin Luther.

8 Read the "Ninety-Five Theses."

9 Do a creative writing exercise on the Counter-Reformation.

10 Do a descriptive writing exercise about the trial of Martin Luther.

11 Conduct read-alouds from *The Prince* by Machiavelli.

12 Read about the execution of Sir Thomas Moore.

Logical/Mathematical

1 List and organize the practices of the Catholic church before the Reformation.

2 Sequence the major events of the Reformation.

3 Compare and contrast the Reformation and Counter-Reformation.

4 Analyze information about the Act of Supremacy in England.

5 Brainstorm ideas about how Jews were treated during the Reformation.

6 Synthesize ideas about the artists of the Renaissance.

7 Compare and contrast two sculptures by Michelangelo.

8 Discover trends in Michelangelo's painting of the Sistine Chapel.

9 Make associations between Michelangelo and Raphael.

10 Solve the problems that Michelangelo faced in painting the Sistine Chapel.

11 List and organize facts about da Vinci's *The Last Supper*.

Adventures Through World History! • Rickey Millwood

Visual/Spatial

1 Watch the movie *The Agony the Ecstasy*.

2 View on the Internet a scene of Michelangelo's painting in the Sistine Chapel.

3 Create a PowerPoint displaying the works of four Renaissance artists.

4 Pretend you are an artist from the Renaissance and discuss your painting techniques.

5 Create a montage about Leonardo da Vinci.

6 Create a political cartoon about the selling of indulgences.

7 Create a political cartoon about Martin Luther.

8 Draw a scene from the Thirty Year's War.

9 Create a graphic organizer about the causes of the Reformation.

10 Create a chart that displays the spreading of the Reformation across Europe.

11 Draw a scene of Charles V during the Reformation.

Musical/Rhythmic

1 Identify the musical instruments from the Renaissance that evolved into modern instruments.

2 Play an instrument from the Renaissance period before the class.

3 Evaluate the changes in Renaissance music from the medieval period.

4 Find pictures on the Internet of instruments from the Renaissance.

5 Look for themes in Renaissance music.

6 Research the major musical composers of the Renaissance.

7 Research songs written by Martin Luther.

8 Determine how music played and sung by Protestants encouraged revolution against the Catholic church.

9 Analyze and determine how the lyrics of the song "A Mighty Fortress Is Our God" by Martin Luther applies to the Reformation.

10 Listen to music from the Renaissance and Reformation.

Chapter 6 continued
The Renaissance and the Reformation (1300—1600)

Bodily/Kinesthetic

1 Build a clay model of a statue sculpted by Michelangelo.

2 Visit the Sistine Chapel on the Internet.

3 Perform a skit about the life of an artist from the Renaissance.

4 Create a Renaissance fair or festival.

5 Act out the role of any Renaissance artist discussing your latest work of art.

6 Re-enact Luther's posting of the "Ninety-Five Theses."

7 Re-create the trial of Sir Thomas Moore.

8 As a class, attend a play written by William Shakespeare.

9 Build a model of the Globe Theater.

10 Visit the Wittenberg Church where Luther posted his "Ninety-Five Theses."

Naturalist

1 Visit Florence, Italy, on the Internet.

2 Examine photos of marble used for sculpting.

3 Visit a park that contains statues designed like those from the Renaissance period.

4 List the major characteristics of Renaissance paintings.

5 Attend a Shakespearean play performed outdoors.

6 Determine how paint was created during the Renaissance.

7 Visit the church in Wittenberg where Luther nailed up his "Ninety-Five Theses."

8 List the characteristics of Gutenberg's printing press.

9 Visit a museum that displays art from the Renaissance.

10 Identify the materials used to create musical instruments during the Renaissance.

Interpersonal

1 Role-play Johann Tetzel selling indulgences across Europe.

2 Role-play Martin Luther protesting the selling of indulgences.

3 Practice taking turns discussing the causes that led to the Reformation.

4 Reach a consensus explaining why a Counter-Reformation took place.

5 Debate the writings and views of Machiavelli in *The Prince*.

6 Discuss with a classmate the mystery behind the *Mona Lisa*.

7 Do a team presentation on the works of four major Renaissance artists.

8 Have students play musical instruments before the class that originated during the Renaissance.

9 Plan a theme or event centered on the Renaissance.

10 Interview other classmates about the role that religion played in Renaissance art.

11 Reach a consensus explaining why Renaissance artists patterned their sculptures from the Classical periods.

12 Take the role as a group of tourists planning a trip to Florence, Italy, to examine Renaissance art.

Intrapersonal

1 Express your likes and dislikes about Renaissance art.

2 Take a stance to protest the selling of indulgences.

3 Take a stance to defend the actions of Martin Luther in posting the "Ninety-Five Theses."

4 Defend the actions of Charles V as he placed Luther on trial.

5 Weigh alternatives to the Spanish Inquisition.

6 Write a code of ethical treatment during the Inquisition.

7 Write about the actions of St. Ignatius of Loyola during the Counter-Reformation.

8 Observe the mood changes in Europeans as a result of the Reformation.

9 Write about the actions of King Henry VIII during the Reformation.

10 Describe your feelings about the political and religious turmoil caused by the Reformation.

The Renaissance and the Reformation

The Protestant Reformation

Martin Luther challenged many practices of the Catholic church such as the selling of indulgences and the supreme power of the Pope. Luther was eventually summoned by Emperor Charles V to Worms, Germany. Luther was instructed to abandon his teachings but refused to recant on the statements he had written against the Catholic church. Luther had come into open rebellion against the practices of the Catholic church.

Others before Luther had been burned at the stake for rebellion. However, the time was right for the Reformation. Luther gained many supporters in Germany, including wealthy princes. These princes despised sending their money to the Catholic church in Rome. To the Princes, Lutheranism was the better choice because these teachings gave them an opportunity to object to the power of the Pope.

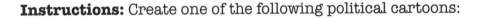

Instructions: Create one of the following political cartoons:

Luther viewed as an enemy of the Catholic church **or** Luther viewed as the champion of the Protestant Reformation

The Renaissance and the Reformation

The Counter-Reformation

The Catholic Church, alarmed by the rapid spread of Protestantism, took measures to slow the followers of Luther and to regain their supporters. These measures included the founding of the Jesuits by Loyola, which spread Catholic teachings, and a cleansing of questionable church practices. The Catholic Church began to punish members for those practices not in line with its teachings and policies.

The Counter-Reformation was successful in checking the expansion of the Protestantism, but Europe was clearly split between the two sects. The nations in Northern Europe were the strongholds for Protestantism while the nations of Southern Europe remained Catholic.

Instructions: In an essay, describe your feelings about the practices of the Catholic church to halt the spread of Protestantism through a Counter-Reformation.

The Renaissance and the Reformation

The Giants of Renaissance Art

When we think of the Renaissance, two men stand above all others. These are Leonardo da Vinci and Michelangelo. Da Vinci was an artist, inventor, and engineer. He was truly a man that could have been an modern inventor in society. His pictures of weapons, parachutes, and flying machines are 500 years ahead of his time. He is also remembered for his painting of the *Mona Lisa* and *The Last Supper*.

Michelangelo—a poet, sculptor, and artist is remembered for his sculptures of *David* and the *Pieta*. He once remarked that he could see figures embedded in marble, so he merely chipped away at the marble until the figured appeared. His most magnificent painting is on the ceiling of the Sistine Chapel. There, for several years, he painted scenes from the Bible while laying on his back, high on a scaffold.

NEWS

Instructions: Write a newspaper article about the completion of one of the great works of either da Vinci or Michelangelo.

The Renaissance and the Reformation

The Printing Press

The single most important invention during the period of the Reformation was moveable type and a newer printing press by Johannes Gutenberg. This invention made it possible for ideas to spread quickly. It allowed for the mass production of books, including the Bible.

It could be argued that the printing press is the most important invention in all of history because it made books widely available and the cost of books dropped to affordable prices. It also allowed individuals to spread their ideas quickly. The printing press gave Martin Luther the technology to spread his ideas throughout Europe.

Instructions: Research the Gutenberg press. Write an instruction manual for the press crew.

Chapter 7: The Age of Discovery (1450—1750)

The Age of Discovery, or the Age of Exploration is one of the most important periods in all of European history. A tremendous amount of knowledge was gained from Europe's expansion across the globe. Europeans learned of new people, plants, and animals from this exploration.

This period of expansion began as a result of the Turks closing the land trade routes to Asia. Europeans, deprived of spices and cargo from the East, turned to the oceans as an attempt to find a westward water passage to Asia. The Catholic church fully supported this exploration and saw this expansion as an opportunity to convert the ungodly to Christians. European monarchs supported this exploration and colonization as they expanded their empires to gain prestige and wealth.

Verbal/Linguistic

1 Write a book report about a Spanish or Portuguese explorer during the Age of Discovery.

2 Write a play or skit about Christopher Columbus.

3 Write a newspaper article about the voyage of Ferdinand Magellan.

4 Share ideas about the reasons the Age of Discovery began.

5 Do a creative writing exercise about the exchange or trade between the Old and New Worlds.

6 Debate the treatment of Native Americans in the New World.

7 Write a narrative about Prince Henry of Portugal.

8 Do a descriptive writing exercise about the first voyage made by Christopher Columbus.

9 Explain the concept "Gold, Glory, and God."

10 Keep a journal or diary as if you were a sailor on a great sea voyage.

Logical/Mathematical

1 Graph the world's population between the years 1450 and 1750.

2 Analyze the data that illustrates what happened to the Native Americans of the New World after 1492.

3 Discover patterns in European expansion.

4 Calculate the mineral wealth extracted from the New World after 1492.

5 List and organize facts about triangular trade.

6 Synthesize ideas about the African slave trade.

7 Make predictions as to what would happen to the Native Americans after small pox was introduced into their cultures.

8 Sequence the major events of the Age of Discovery between 1492 and 1750.

9 Compare and contrast European medicine with Inca medicine.

10 Calculate the probability of the English defeating the Spanish Armada in 1588.

Adventures Through World History! • Rickey Millwood
Kagan Publishing • 1 (800) 933-2667 • www.KaganOnline.com

Visual/Spatial

1 Draw a scene depicting the world as flat and the oceans filled with sea monsters.

2 Create a map of the world in 1750.

3 Chart the route of a famous European navigator.

4 Design a postcard about the Age of Discovery.

5 Draw a scene about Hernando Cortés and the Aztecs.

6 Design an outfit worn by a Spanish conquistador.

7 Draw a scene about the defeat of the Spanish Armada.

8 Make a sculpture of the Mayan pyramids at Chichen Itza.

9 Draw a scene of a Mayan ball game at Chichen Itza.

10 Imagine you were with Francisco Pizarro as he entered the Inca Empire.

11 Create a PowerPoint about five European explorers and their voyages.

12 Design a book cover about the Age of Discovery.

Musical/Rhythmic

1 Evaluate the impact that African music had upon the New World.

2 Write a song about the Aztecs, Mayans, or Incas.

3 Compose a melody about Prince Henry the Navigator.

4 Write a song about the defeat of the Spanish Armada.

5 Write a rap song about Christopher Columbus.

6 Learn about the instruments played by the Mayans and Aztecs.

7 Perform a dance before the class as performed by the Mayans.

8 Learn about musical instruments that came from Africa to the New World.

9 Listen to calypso music.

10 Report on the musical instruments played on long sea voyages.

Chapter 7 continued
The Age of Discovery
(1450–1750)

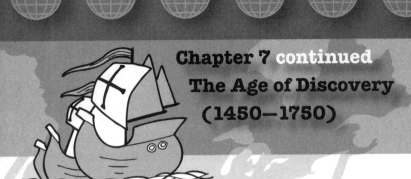

Bodily/Kinesthetic

1 Perform a skit about the Age of Discovery.

2 Build a model of a European caravel.

3 Build a model of Tenochtitlan, the Aztec capital.

4 Visit St. Augustine, Florida, and the Fountain of Youth.

5 Create a project displaying the different foods that Europeans discovered in America.

6 Create a display of African crops taken to the New World.

7 Create a menu of European foods consumed before the Age of Discovery.

8 Use physical gestures that would have been exchanged between Native Americans and Europeans.

9 Visit Chichen Itza, Mexico, on the Internet.

10 Build a model of a Mayan pyramid.

11 Build a model of an astrolabe, quadrant, or sextant.

Naturalist

1 Record the ecological changes in the New World after Europeans arrived.

2 Observe the materials Native Americans used for housing materials.

3 Observe building materials used in Mayan architecture.

4 Categorize the natural materials the Mayans used for medical purposes.

5 List the animals in the New World never seen by Europeans.

6 Categorize the animals that Europeans brought to the New World.

7 Record the changes in the population of Africa during the Age of Discovery.

8 Observe the solar system and determine how captains navigated by the celestial bodies.

9 Record the materials used to build ships such as the caravel.

10 Record the changes in ship construction as the Age of Discovery progressed.

11 Observe the differences between materials used for Native Americans and European clothing.

12 List the characteristics of the weapons used by the Aztecs.

13 Compile data about the aviary in Tenochtitlan, the Aztec capital.

Interpersonal

1 Plan an event about Columbus Day.

2 Debate the treatment of Native Americans in the New World.

3 Discuss with a partner the impact of the slave trade between Europe and Africa.

4 Reach a consensus on the impact that disease had upon the Native Americans.

5 Mediate the conflict between Cortés and Montezuma.

6 Solve the problems that European captains faced as they made long sea voyages.

7 Discuss with a partner the importance of the voyage made by Magellan.

8 Reach a consensus on how the world changed during the Age of Exploration.

9 Interview classmates about the Age of Discovery.

10 Share with others information about the movement of plants and animals from one continent to another.

11 Role-play a survivor from the conquest of Tenochtitlan.

12 Do a team presentation on the causes and the effects of the Age of Exploration.

Intrapersonal

1 Think about the actions of the Spanish conquistadors.

2 Describe your feelings about the Atlantic slave trade.

3 Describe your feelings about the impact that disease had upon Native Americans of the New World.

4 Express your likes and dislikes about European conquistadors.

5 Write a code of conduct for the treatment of Native Americans in the New World.

6 Prioritize items needed for a long sea voyage.

7 Observe the mood changes in European monarchs after 1492.

8 Weigh alternatives to the destruction of Tenochtitlan by Hernando Cortés.

9 Take a stance to defend the action of Spain in 1588 to invade England.

10 Express your likes and dislikes about Francis Drake.

11 Think about the actions of the conquistadors as they plundered the New World.

12 Choose between the alternatives of going on a sea voyage or remaining in Europe.

Adventures Through World History!
Kagan Publishing • 1 (800) 933-2667 • www.KaganOnline.com

7.1 Blackline Master • Naturalist Activities

The Age of Discovery

The Beginning of World Trade

The Age of Exploration opened the world of trade between nations. Goods were exchanged between the regions of Europe, Asia, Africa, and America. A major part of this trade involved the movement of plants and foods to different regions of the globe.

The movement of crops helped eliminate famines and allowed for a more nutritious diet. The world's population doubled during the Age of Exploration; a major reason for the increase was the fact that crops were exchanged between four major regions.

Activity Options

1. Research the origin of several major foods that were exchanged between the continents from 1450 to 1750. Create a display of foods on four tables that demonstrate the major crops that originated in Europe, Africa, America, or Asia prior to the Age of Exploration.

2. Determine the nutritional value of the major foods that were exchanged between the four regions.

_____
_____
_____
_____
_____
_____
_____
_____
_____
_____
_____
_____

Adventures Through World History! • Rickey Millwood
Kagan Publishing • 1 (800) 933-2667 • www.KaganOnline.com

7.2 Blackline Master • Logical/Mathematical Activity

The Age of Discovery

The Impact of Disease upon the New World

The Spanish conquistadors brought many diseases to the New World that decimated the Native Americans. The Native Americans had no immunity to these new diseases such as plague, measles, influenza, small pox, and tuberculosis. Certainly, these infectious diseases claimed more lives than did Spanish weapons. The Native Americans had no antibodies or medications, such as antibiotics, to fight off these diseases. Thus, Native Americans died by the millions in the century following the first voyage of Columbus.

Instructions: Throughout history, mankind has battled epidemics. We face some of the same diseases spread by the conquistadors. Make predictions about current diseases and how they are affecting the world today. Make your predictions about what the future holds for the following diseases and the impact they will have within the next 50 years.

Avian Bird Flu _____
_____

Ebola _____
_____

West Nile Virus _____
_____

Malaria _____
_____

AIDS _____
_____

Tuberculosis _____
_____

Adventures Through World History! • Rickey Millwood
Kagan Publishing • 1 (800) 933-2667 • www.KaganOnline.com

7.3 Blackline Master • Intrapersonal Activity

The Age of Discovery

Dangerous Sea Voyages

Sea captains often had a difficult time trying to round up a crew for long sea voyages. Many potential sailors were terrified of myths and refused to even consider going to sea. Stories about the earth being flat and the oceans being filled with sea dragons played on the imaginations of many sailors.

These voyages could last up to a year and were extremely challenging. Sailors faced rough seas, shipwreck, starvation, and nasty conditions on the ships. Mutiny was always a possibility. Yet these brave men sailed with famous captains, such as Vasco da Gama, Christopher Columbus, and Ferdinand Magellan, in an attempt to strike it rich or just for the thrill of adventure.

Instructions: Make a journal entry as if you were a sailor with Vasco da Gama or Ferdinand Magellan as he made a historical sea voyage. Be sure to include a thrilling or dramatic moment in your entry.

The Age of Discovery

The Defeat of the Spanish Armada

In 1588, Spain attempted to invade England for several reasons. England and Spain were bitter rivals as England had split with the Catholic church, and both nations were in competition for colonies and empires in the New World.

Sir Francis Drake of England led raids and captured Spanish treasure ships, which infuriated the Spanish. The English viewed Drake as a hero while the Spanish viewed him as a pirate. In 1588, the Spanish Armada attempted to crush England but it was the Armada that suffered a staggering defeat.

Spain lost its military power, and England gained colonies along the Atlantic seaboard in America. England had triumphed over the Armada with its smaller but faster naval fleet. This was a turning point in naval warfare and in European history.

Instructions: Compare and contrast the English navy with the Spanish Armada.

English Navy | **Spanish Armada**

Chapter 8
The Advanced Civilizations of Mexico and Peru
(500–1550)

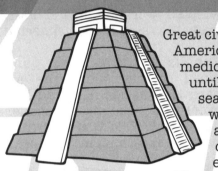

Great civilizations flourished in the region we know as Latin America. These civilizations were highly advanced in architecture, medicine, and agricultural practices. These societies prospered until the arrival of the Spanish conquistadors who came in search of the gold. These societies had never been in contact with the diseases from Europe and perished by the millions after the arrival of the Spanish. Spain established new colonies and built an empire in the New World. Treasure extracted from these civilizations made Spain the most prosperous nation in the world.

Verbal/Linguistic

1 Do a descriptive writing exercise about the Mayan city of Chichen Itza.

2 Compare and contrast Mayan and Inca architecture.

3 Write a newspaper article about the arrival of the Spanish conquistador Hernando Cortés to the New World.

4 Compare and contrast the religious views of the Spanish and Aztecs.

5 Share ideas about the superstition of the Aztecs.

6 Write a poem about the Aztec chief Montezuma.

7 Read about Aztec sacrifices and superstitions.

8 Write a letter about the destruction of Tenochtitlan, the Aztec capital.

9 Read about Francisco Pizarro's invasion of the Inca Empire.

10 Do a descriptive writing exercise about the death of Atahualpa, the Inca emperor.

11 Tell about the major advancements of the Maya, Aztecs, and Incas.

Logical/Mathematical

1 Make predictions about the outcome of the collision between the Aztecs and Spanish.

2 Use inductive reasoning to determine how the Spanish were able to defeat the Aztecs.

3 Make a graph illustrating the decline of the Native American population in America from 1492-1650.

4 Discover trends in the agricultural practices of the Mayans and Incas.

5 Sequence the events on a time line of the fall of the Aztec and Inca empires.

6 Discover patterns in the Spanish treatment of the Native Americans in the New World.

7 Do calculations to determine the amount of gold and silver the Spanish extracted from the New World.

8 Compare and contrast the Mayan pyramids at Chichen Itza with Egyptian pyramids.

Adventures Through World History! • Rickey Millwood
Kagan Publishing • 1 (800) 933-2667 • www.KaganOnline.com

Visual/Spatial

1 Build a model of the Mayan pyramids at Chichen Itza.

2 Build a model of the great ball court at Chichen Itza.

3 Create an illustration of Tenochtitlan.

4 Draw a scene about the Aztecs.

5 Pretend you were a Spanish soldier entering the Aztec empire with Cortés.

6 Draw a scene of the conquest of the Aztec Empire.

7 Draw a scene depicting the spread of disease in the New World.

8 Draw a scene about the death of Atahualpa, the Inca emperor.

9 Watch a film about the fall of the Aztecs or Incas.

10 Design a postcard about the architecture of the Mayans or Incas.

11 Chart the route of Inca relay runners through the Andes Mountains.

12 Examine pictures of Cuzco and Chichen Itza on the Internet.

13 Examine a drawing of Quetzalcoatl, the god of the Aztecs.

14 Examine pictures of quipus.

15 Diagram Spanish weapons.

Musical/Rhythmic

1 Learn about the musical instruments of the Mayans, Aztecs, and Incas.

2 Study about the importance of dance in the Aztec society.

3 Determine the relationship between dance and religion in the Mayan, Aztec, and Inca cultures.

4 Compose a melody about the sacrifices of the Aztecs.

5 Write a song about Hernando Cortés.

6 Compare and contrast the music of the Spanish and Aztecs.

7 Write a jingle about the superstition of the Aztecs.

8 Evaluate the importance and influence of music on the young warriors in the Aztec society.

9 Build an instrument similar to those played by the Mayans or Aztecs.

Adventures Through World History! • Rickey Millwood
Kagan Publishing • 1 (800) 933-2667 • www.KaganOnline.com

Chapter 8 continued
The Advanced Civilizations of Mexico and Peru (500—1550)

Bodily/Kinesthetic

1 Act out the role of an Inca relay runner.

2 Build a model of the pyramid at Chichen Itza.

3 Create a display of the major foods eaten by the Mayans and Incas.

4 Act out the role of a Spanish soldier entering the Aztec empire.

5 Create musical instruments played by the Aztecs.

6 Re-create a Mayan ball game.

7 Visit Tulum, Chichen Itza, or Cuzco.

8 Perform a skit about the Spanish conquistadors.

9 Create a display of food crops the Spanish brought to the New World.

10 Interview a physician about the impact of new diseases that were brought to the New World.

Naturalist

1 Learn about the region of Chichen Itza, Mexico.

2 Classify the natural materials used for the construction of Mayan pyramids.

3 Categorize the materials used to build Aztec weapons.

4 Learn of the importance of the sun to the Aztecs.

5 Examine photographs of the jungles of the Yucatán Peninsula.

6 Record the changes in the developmental stages of the Aztec capital.

7 List the characteristics of Lake Texcoco.

8 Identify the symbols on the flag of Mexico.

9 Determine the importance of shellfish in the diet of the Mayans.

10 List the various pets of the Aztecs.

11 Identify animals the Spanish had never seen until their arrival in America.

12 Identify the various types of livestock the Spanish brought to America.

13 Identify the materials used by the Incas to create quipus for record keeping.

14 List facts about the foods consumed by the Mayans and Aztecs.

Adventures Through World History! • Rickey Millwood
Kagan Publishing • 1 (800) 933-2667 • www.KaganOnline.com

Interpersonal

1 Do team presentations on the Mayans, Aztecs, and Incas.

2 Share with others the religious views of the Mayans and Aztecs.

3 Role-play Spanish soldiers entering the Aztec empire.

4 Role-play Aztecs in their first encounter with the Spanish.

5 Interview other classmates about the diseases the Spanish brought to the New World.

6 Discuss with a partner the major reasons why the Spanish desired to conquer the inhabitants of Mexico.

7 Reach a consensus explaining why the outnumbered Spaniards were able to conquer the Aztecs and Incas.

8 Discuss the role that religion played in the conquest of the Aztecs and Incas.

9 Practice taking turns telling how superstition contributed to the downfall of the Aztecs.

10 Share with others evidence that proves the Incas were a highly advanced civilization.

11 In pairs, determine how the Mayan, Aztec, and Inca civilizations made major contributions to the modern world.

Intrapersonal

1 Defend or deny the position that the Spanish had the right to conquer and subjugate the Aztecs and Incas.

2 Describe your feelings about Aztec sacrifices.

3 Describe your feelings about the architectural advances of the Mayans and Incas.

4 Form an action plan the Aztecs and Incas could have employed to have defeated Cortés and Pizarro.

5 Observe the mood changes in Spain after the conquest of Mexico.

6 Write an ethical code of treatment for the Aztecs and Incas who survived the Spanish conquest.

7 Choose between being an Aztec, Inca, or Mayan citizen as the Spanish arrived. Explain your reasons for your choice.

8 Make a journal entry as if you were a Spanish soldier with Cortés or Pizarro.

9 Think about the actions used by the Spanish to capture and hold Montezuma.

10 Write a personal poem about Montezuma or Atahualpa.

11 Weigh alternatives to the destruction of the Aztec capital of Tenochtitlan.

12 Think about the importance of architecture and science to the Mayans.

8.1 Blackline Master • Bodily/Kinesthetic Activity

The Advanced Civilizations of Mexico and Peru

A Collision of Cultures

The Spanish conquistadors must have stood in awe of the great Aztec Empire. This civilization was much more advanced than the Spanish had ever dreamed. The architecture and wealth of the Aztecs was breathtaking. Surely the treasure the Spanish were seeking could be found in this empire.

The Aztecs outnumbered the Spanish, but the desire for gold overcame any fear. The Spanish had horses, muskets, and swords. In addition, the Spanish played upon Aztec superstition. Furthermore, the Spanish infected the Aztecs with deadly microbes such as smallpox.

Instructions: Form small groups. Tell the class that they are Spanish conquistadors who will fight the Aztecs. Have them role-play a discussion about their forthcoming attack. Groups can share their skits with another group or with the entire class. Here are some ideas they can discuss:

- the fact that the Spanish are far outnumbered
- the Aztecs engage in human sacrifices
- the Aztec capital is built on an island in a lake
- the Aztecs have a strong ruler in Montezuma
- the Spanish have horses, guns, and cannons
- Hernando Cortés has burned his own ships and the Spanish soldiers have no way of escape

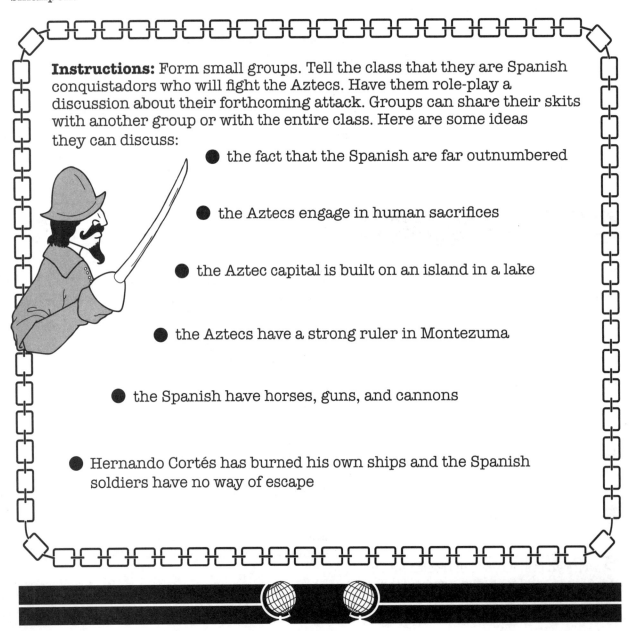

Adventures Through World History! • Rickey Millwood
Kagan Publishing • 1 (800) 933-2667 • www.KaganOnline.com

8.2 Blackline Master • Interpersonal Activity

The Advanced Civilizations of Mexico and Peru

The Conquest of the Incas

After conquering the Aztecs, the Spanish headed for Peru and Bolivia. This region was home to the mighty Inca Empire. The Spanish conquistadors were brutal in their treatment of the Incas. They justified their treatment of the Indians by stating that they had a Christian duty to civilize these savage people.

The Spanish murdered the Inca Chief Atahualpa after he had paid a huge ransom to spare his life. Then, they burned his body. To the Incas, this meant his soul was lost.

These conquistadors were ruthless. Nothing stood in their way to control Incas or their vast empire. Incas who survived the conquest were forced into slavery and made to dig silver and gold from the mines.

Instructions: Conduct a trial and charge Spanish conquistador Francisco Pizarro with crimes against humanity due to savage treatment of the Incas. On a separate sheet of paper, write the transcript from the trial. Determine who will play the different roles.

Francisco Pizarro _____

Prosecution Team _____

Incas _____

Defense Team _____

Spanish Soldiers _____

Jury _____

Judge _____

Adventures Through World History! • Rickey Millwood
Kagan Publishing • 1 (800) 933-2667 • www.KaganOnline.com

8.3 Blackline Master • Verbal/Linguistic Activity

The Advanced Civilizations of Mexico and Peru

Letters from a Conquistador

Imagine being a Spanish soldier who served under Cortés or Pizarro. You would have witnessed the destruction of two major civilizations in Mexico and Peru. These empires were powerful and rich in treasure. The Incas and Aztecs had weapons, but they were no match for military and biological weapons used by the Spanish. You would have witnessed two highly advanced civilizations obliterated by Spain because of greed.

Instructions: Write a letter to your family back in Spain as if you were a conquistador. Vividly describe the conquest of either the Aztecs or Incas.

8.4 Blackline Master • Logical/Mathematical Activity

The Advanced Civilizations of Mexico and Peru

Mayan Architecture

The great Mayan city of Chichen Itza demonstrates the architectural genius of this civilization. These ruins contain evidence of a civilization that was highly skilled in mathematics and engineering. These buildings and structures are unbelievable, considering they were built over 1,000 years ago. There is an observatory, ball court, and the great pyramid of Kukulan (El Castillo). The pyramid is perfect in shape and contains a total of 365 steps, one step for each day of the year. Today, the ruins of Chichen Itza are a major attraction to visitors of Cancun, Mexico.

Instructions: Examine pictures of Chichen Itza and Egyptian pyramids on the Internet. Compare and contrast the pyramids using the Venn diagram below.

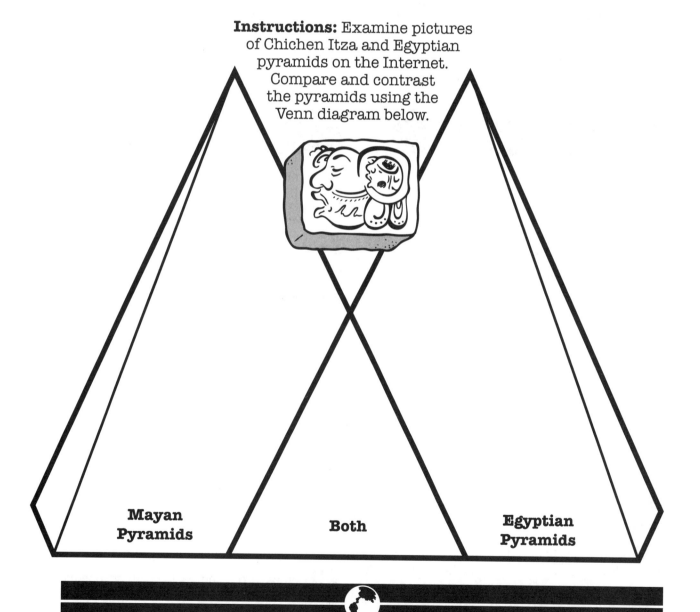

Mayan Pyramids | Both | Egyptian Pyramids

Adventures Through World History! • Rickey Millwood
Kagan Publishing • 1 (800) 933-2667 • www.KaganOnline.com

Chapter 9: The Scientific Revolution and the Enlightenment
(1550–1789)

The Scientific Revolution opened the eyes of Europeans as theories and beliefs from the Middle Ages were disputed and challenged. Scientists and astronomers, such as Copernicus, Kepler, and Galileo, discovered truths through experimentation about our solar system. The belief that Earth was the center of the entire universe was proven to be inaccurate by astronomers. Disputing the beliefs of the Catholic church could get one into a lot of trouble, which was the case for Galileo. Just as astronomers were challenging the church over the laws of the solar system, the concept of divine right of kings would also come into question. The teachings of the philosophers contributed to the Age of Revolution.

Verbal/Linguistic

1. Explain the concept of the scientific method.
2. Compare and contrast the geocentric and heliocentric theories.
3. Write a paper about the views of Nicolaus Copernicus.
4. Write a skit about Galileo's trial.
5. Do a descriptive writing exercise about the discoveries of Galileo.
6. Give a speech as Francis Bacon about scientific reasoning.
7. Discuss the political theories of John Locke.
8. Explain the concept of divine right.
9. Share ideas about the teachings of Voltaire.
10. Read about Louis XIV and his life at Versailles.

Logical/Mathematical

1. List ideas about Copernicus and his views.
2. Create an illustration of Johannes Kepler's view of planets in motion.
3. Conduct an experiment to prove Isaac Newton's law of gravity.
4. Sequence the major events during the Scientific Revolution.
5. Compare and contrast the teachings of anatomy by Andreas Vesalius.
6. List and organize facts about the first telescopes.
7. Evaluate the ideas of blood circulation by William Harvey.
8. Apply medical information learned during the Scientific Revolution to the medical profession today.
9. Explain why the Catholic church attacked the views of Copernicus and Galileo.
10. Compare and contrast the encyclopedia today with Denis Diderot's first version.
11. Test Newton's law of inertia.

Visual/Spatial

1 Examine the artwork of Rembrandt van Rijn.

2 Make a visual aid to explain the laws of Johannes Kepler.

3 Create a ladder graphic organizer demonstrating the major medical advances during the Scientific Revolution.

4 Create an illustration of Andreas Vesalius conducting an experiment in his laboratory.

5 Create a collage of scientists from the Scientific Revolution.

6 Create a chart displaying the advancement of scientific instruments during the Scientific Revolution.

7 Draw a scene of Louis XIV and his view of the divine right of kings.

8 Visualize being a peasant in France during the reign of Louis XIV.

9 Create a scene from the Scientific Revolution or the Enlightenment.

10 Make a poster illustrating the powers of an absolute monarch.

Musical/Rhythmic

1 Listen to the music composed by Johann Sebastian Bach.

2 Listen to music composed by George Frideric Handel.

3 Evaluate the styles of music during the Enlightenment.

4 Discover instruments that were new to the Enlightenment.

5 Listen to European composed music during the Enlightenment.

6 Determine how operas were related to new democratic themes during the Enlightenment.

7 Study how music during the Enlightenment was aimed toward the middle class for entertainment.

8 Write a song about a philosopher during the Enlightenment.

9 Evaluate the impact and influence of Baroque music.

10 Compare and contrast Baroque music with music from the Classical period.

11 Identify the musical instruments heard in Baroque music.

12 Play instruments in the classroom heard in Baroque music.

Adventures Through World History! • Rickey Millwood
Kagan Publishing • 1 (800) 933-2667 • www.KaganOnline.com

Chapter 9 continued
The Scientific Revolution and the Enlightenment (1550–1789)

Bodily/Kinesthetic

1 Act out the role of an astronomer during the Scientific Revolution.

2 Conduct an experiment performed by Isaac Newton.

3 Build a model of a telescope used during the Scientific Revolution.

4 Act out the stages of the scientific method.

5 Perform a skit about Francis Bacon.

6 Research objects dissected by Andreas Vesalius, the father of anatomy.

7 Build a model of a planetarium.

8 Act out the role of John Locke and his opinions of democracy.

9 Perform a skit about life in the Palace of Versailles.

10 Visit a modern hospital laboratory.

11 Act out the role of modern professions based on the work of Vesalius.

12 Create a project to compare and contrast the heliocentric and geocentric theories.

Naturalist

1 Examine the solar system from a planetarium.

2 Observe an eclipse and explain how and why it occurs.

3 List the characteristics of Edmond Halley's comet.

4 Explain how Edmond Halley used the work of Isaac Newton to predict the return of the comet.

5 List the characteristics of the telescope used by Galileo.

6 Note the observations made by Copernicus and Galileo.

7 List the characteristics of the first microscope.

8 Record the discoveries made by Antoni van Leeuwenhoek.

9 Record the discoveries of Antoine Lavoisier.

10 Create an illustration of William Harvey's ideas of blood circulation.

11 Discus natural rights and a primitive state as defined by Jean-Jacques Rousseau.

Interpersonal

1 Discuss with a partner the geocentric theory.

2 Debate why the Catholic church supported a geocentric theory of the solar system.

3 Have classmates interview each other about the steps of the scientific method.

4 Reach a consensus on the importance of the writings of Locke and Rousseau.

5 Share with others your thoughts on the secret work of Vesalius.

6 Practice criticizing the spending habits of Louis XIV, the Sun King.

7 Share with others your feelings about the divine right of kings.

8 Interview each other about the theories of Isaac Newton.

9 Role-play major characters from the Scientific Revolution as if they were conducting a news conference.

10 Take the role of Galileo and defend the heliocentric theory of the solar system.

11 Plan an event about the music of the Enlightenment.

12 Do a team presentation on the major composers during the Enlightenment.

Intrapersonal

1 Write about the actions of some of the famous astronomers and their discoveries during the Scientific Revolution.

2 Reflect on the knowledge acquired by scientists during the Scientific Revolution.

3 Describe your feelings about the resistance men of science faced from Catholic church officials.

4 Think about the actions of kings claiming to have divine right.

5 Describe your feelings about the philosophers during the Enlightenment.

6 Write about the needs of the common people during the Enlightenment.

7 Express your likes and dislikes about Baroque music.

8 Meditate on how the Enlightenment led to the Age of Revolution against established monarchs.

9 Choose between living in France or England in 1650 and explain your reasons.

10 Defend the actions by Voltaire to condemn trial and persecution by religious authorities.

11 List and analyze the top priorities of King Louis XIV.

12 Respond to the hypothetical dilemma of having a king rule the United States.

9.1 Blackline Master • Logical/Mathematical Activity

The Scientific Revolution and the Enlightenment

Challenging Accepted Medical Opinion

Andreas Vesalius, considered the father of human anatomy, removed corpses from cemeteries and gallows to examine the physical workings of the body. Imagine the stories that circulated about his medical interests! Fascinated by the actual mechanics of human organs, Versalius dissected these bodies to acquire accurate information. He was trying to disprove the theories of Galen, a Greek physician, who often worked with animals and incorrectly believed that the organs of animals were identical to those of humans. Vesalius' methods were frowned upon by many, but eventually he became the physician of Charles V, Holy Roman Emperor.

Instructions: Compare and contrast the ideas about human anatomy of Galen with those of Vesalius.

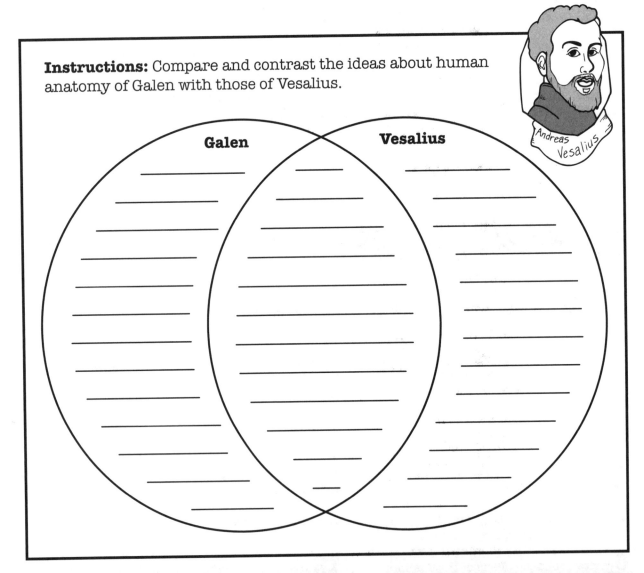

Adventures Through World History! • **Rickey Millwood**
Kagan Publishing • 1 (800) 933-2667 • www.KaganOnline.com

The Scientific Revolution and the Enlightenment

An Innocent Man Stands Trial

As we have seen in previous chapters, challenging Catholic church policies could quickly get one into serious trouble. Such was the fate of Galileo, an Italian astronomer and inventor. Galileo publicly stated his views about the motions of planets.

Galileo knew the planets, including Earth, revolve around the sun. The church believed that God had placed man on Earth, and therefore Earth was indeed the center of the entire universe. Galileo was placed on trial for challenging the beliefs and authority of the church.

People were burned at the stake for saying much less than Galileo. Would Galileo persist and hold to his discoveries and risk execution? Fearing for his life, when Galileo was 70, he agreed to give up his teachings.

Instructions: Re-create the trial of Galileo. Include the following elements:

- Geocentric theory of the universe
- Medieval view of the universe
- Heliocentric theory of the universe

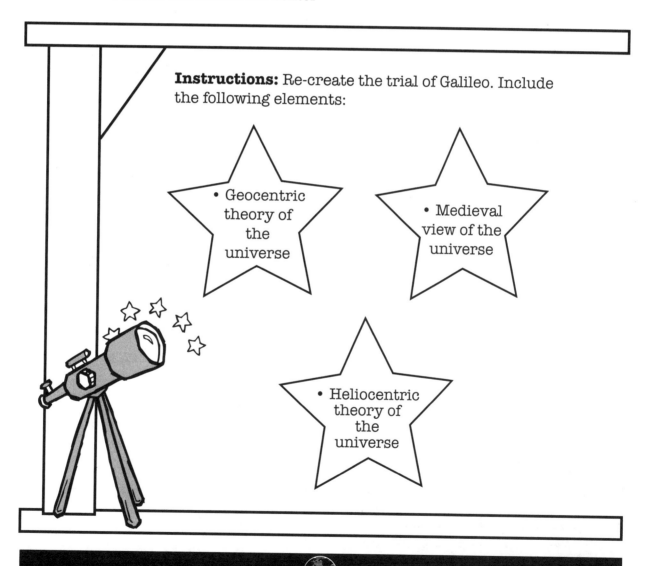

9.3 Blackline Master • Visual/Spatial Activity

The Scientific Revolution and the Enlightenment

The Enlightenment

The Enlightenment, or Age of Reason, followed the Scientific Revolution. If man could seek the truth about the laws of nature, then why could man not question political thought? The Enlightenment brought back the concept of democracy from ancient Greece, and philosophers challenged the belief in the divine right of kings. There is little doubt that the writings of the philosophers contributed to the revolutions in England, America, and France. The philosophers made further contributions by making society aware of foolish superstitions. Voltaire poked fun at established traditions and religion through his sharp satires. These philosophers desired to bring forth truthful information, based on scientific fact—not superstition. Perhaps the greatest source of accurate information came from Denis Diderot and his new encyclopedia.

Instructions: Create a word search about the Enlightenment.

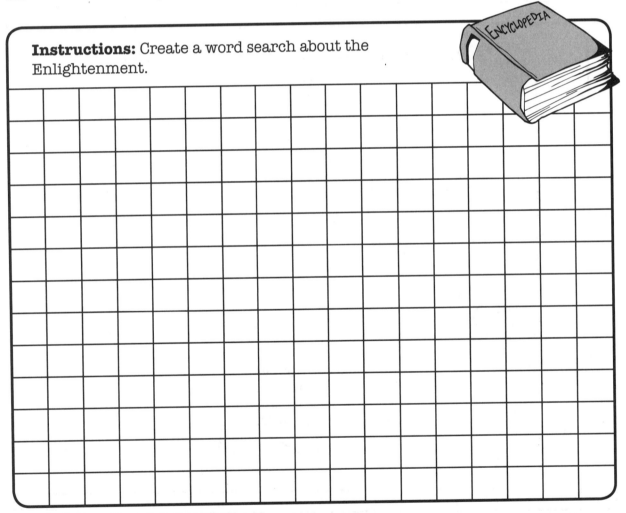

Adventures Through World History! • Rickey Millwood
Kagan Publishing • 1 (800) 933-2667 • www.KaganOnline.com

9.4 Blackline Master • Musical/Rhythmic Activities

The Scientific Revolution and the Enlightenment

A New Style of Music

Just as the Renaissance produced magnificent artists, such as daVinci and Michelangelo, the Enlightenment produced two of the greatest musical composers of all time. Johann Sebastian Bach and George Frideric Handel produced musical compositions in a new style of music, which became known as Baroque.

This music was to entertain the masses, but it sometimes had religious overtones. Clearly this music was a break from Renaissance music. This musical style fits between the Renaissance period and Classical period that followed.

Activity Options

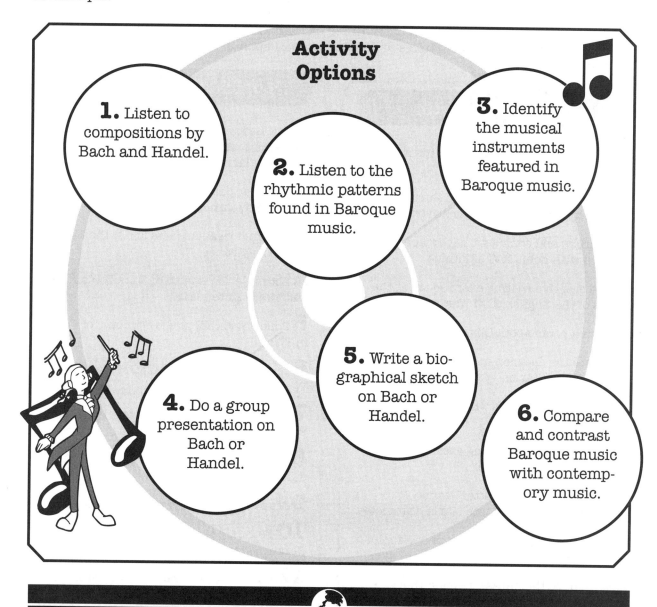

1. Listen to compositions by Bach and Handel.
2. Listen to the rhythmic patterns found in Baroque music.
3. Identify the musical instruments featured in Baroque music.
4. Do a group presentation on Bach or Handel.
5. Write a biographical sketch on Bach or Handel.
6. Compare and contrast Baroque music with contempory music.

Adventures Through World History! • Rickey Millwood
Kagan Publishing • 1 (800) 933-2667 • www.KaganOnline.com

Chapter 10: The Age of Democratic Revolution (1640–1830)

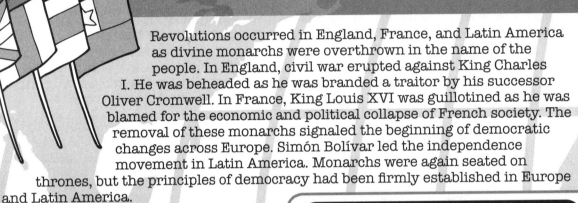

Revolutions occurred in England, France, and Latin America as divine monarchs were overthrown in the name of the people. In England, civil war erupted against King Charles I. He was beheaded as he was branded a traitor by his successor Oliver Cromwell. In France, King Louis XVI was guillotined as he was blamed for the economic and political collapse of French society. The removal of these monarchs signaled the beginning of democratic changes across Europe. Simón Bolívar led the independence movement in Latin America. Monarchs were again seated on thrones, but the principles of democracy had been firmly established in Europe and Latin America.

Verbal/Linguistic

1. Explain the concept of the divine right of kings.
2. Write a letter in the role of a Puritan telling why you are moving to America.
3. Compare and contrast Charles I of England with Louis XVI of France.
4. Do a creative writing exercise about the causes of the English Civil War.
5. Write a poem about Oliver Cromwell.
6. Debate the decision by Oliver Cromwell to execute King Charles.
7. Discuss the reasons why the French Revolution occurred.
8. Do a descriptive writing exercise about the attack on the Bastille.
9. Write a persuasive letter urging Robespierre not to execute Marie Antoinette.
10. Write a biographical sketch of Napoléon Bonaparte.
11. Analyze the phrase, "Honor, Glory, Riches."

Logical/Mathematical

1. Estimate the number of Puritans who migrated to America while King Charles I ruled England.
2. Discover patterns in the English and French Revolutions.
3. List and organize facts about the Three Estates of France.
4. Estimate the wealth of King Louis XVI and Marie Antoinette.
5. Collect data about the economy of France in 1789.
6. Organize facts about the Palace of Versailles.
7. Sequence the major events during the French Revolution.
8. Estimate how many Frenchmen died during the Reign of Terror.
9. Map Napoléon's invasion of Russia.
10. Estimate the number of soldiers Napoléon lost in Russia.
11. Use inductive reasoning to determine why Napoléon's invasion of Russia miserably failed.

Visual/Spatial

1 Watch the film *Cromwell*.

2 Examine political cartoons about the French Revolution.

3 Make a graphic organizer that illustrates the causes and effects of the French Revolution.

4 Visualize attending the execution of King Louis XVI.

5 Create an illustration about the guillotine.

6 Make a poster that presents facts about the guillotine.

7 Draw a scene about the death of Marie Antoinette.

8 Imagine you were living in France during the Reign of Terror.

9 Watch the film *The Guillotine*.

10 Watch the film *A Tale of Two Cities*.

11 Design a winter scene about Napoléon's excursion into Russia.

12 Design a scene about Napoléon while he was on the island of St. Helena.

13 View on the Internet 10 famous paintings of Napoléon Bonaparte.

14 View the chess set of Napoléon Bonaparte at the Biltmore Castle in Asheville, North Carolina.

Musical/Rhythmic

1 Listen to an old English song about Oliver Cromwell.

2 Listen to "*La Marseillaise*."

3 Interpret the lyrics to "*La Marseillaise*."

4 Read about Beethoven's Third Symphony and Napoléon Bonaparte.

5 Write a rap song about the guillotine and the Reign of Terror.

6 Write a song about the lifestyle of Marie Antoinette.

7 Learn about the use of musical instruments in the Napolonic Wars.

8 Listen to patriotic French music which was played during Napoléon's campaigns.

9 Write a jingle about Napoléon's disaster in Russia.

10 Listen to any songs about Waterloo.

Adventures Through World History! • Rickey Millwood

Chapter 10 continued
The Age of Democratic Revolution
(1640–1830)

 Bodily/Kinesthetic

1 Act out the role of a Cavalier and explain why you support King Charles.

2 Act out the role of a Roundhead and explain why you oppose King Charles.

3 Role-play Joseph Guillotine and explain your opinion of the death penalty.

4 Act out the role of French citizens from the First, Second, and Third Estates.

5 Act out the role of a French citizen that witnessed the attack on the Bastille.

6 Role-play Robespierre and explain why France needs a Reign of Terror.

7 Act out a member of the aristocracy during the Reign of Terror.

8 Read about French experiments conducted with the guillotine in 1792.

9 Role-play a French soldier that survived the Moscow campaign.

10 Build a model of the Palace of Versailles.

11 Create a class project about the French Revolution.

12 Debate the causes of the French and American Revolutions.

13 Perform a skit about Simon Bolivar's dream of a united South America.

14 Act out the role of Simón Bolívar and José de San Martin the first time they met.

 Naturalist

1 Record the changes in materials used to build forts and castles in the 1600s.

2 List the materials used for weaponry before 1700.

3 Record the changes in ship building by 1750.

4 List the natural materials used to build a guillotine.

5 List the characteristics of a Russian winter.

6 Describe how the extreme climate in Russia affected the French soldiers.

7 Read about the observations made by Napoléon's physician concerning extremely cold temperatures.

8 Read about how the extreme climate affected the horses during the Russian campaign.

9 View a picture of Napoléon's soldiers in a Russian winter.

10 Write about the island of St. Helena, where Napoléon died.

11 Read about Simón Bolívar's campaign through the Andes to defeat the Spanish in Colombia.

Adventures Through World History! • Rickey Millwood
Kagan Publishing • 1 (800) 933-2667 • www.KaganOnline.com

Interpersonal

1 Do a team presentation on the causes of the English Civil War.

2 Share with others your thoughts on the execution of King Charles I.

3 Reach a consensus explaining how Oliver Cromwell became Lord Protector.

4 Interview each other about the Restoration.

5 Debate the humane use of the guillotine.

6 Share with others the causes of the French Revolution.

7 In teams, discuss the major events of the French Revolution.

8 Write a collaborative paper on the Reign of Terror.

9 Discuss with a partner Napoléon Bonaparte's major reforms.

10 Debate the logic of the Continental System.

11 Share with others your thoughts on Napoléon crowning himself emperor.

12 Take turns explaining why Napoléon invaded Russia.

13 Interview classmates about Napoléon's failure to conquer Russia.

14 Reach a consensus why European nations joined together to defeat Napoléon at Waterloo.

15 In pairs, explain why a united South America never came into existence.

Intrapersonal

1 Express your likes and dislikes about Oliver Cromwell.

2 Describe your feelings about the use of the guillotine on a grand scale in France.

3 Defend or condemn the decision to execute Marie Antoinette.

4 Write about the actions of Robespierre during the Reign of Terror.

5 Describe your feelings about Napoléon's overthrow of the French government.

6 Weigh alternatives to the Continental System.

7 Write about the actions of Napoléon when he crowned himself emperor.

8 Condemn Napoléon's decision to invade Russia.

9 Make a journal entry as if you were a French soldier retreating from Russia.

10 Think about the actions the Russians took to drive Napoléon out of their nation.

11 Write a personal poem about Napoléon's defeat at Waterloo.

12 Weigh alternatives to placing a defeated Napoléon on St. Helena Island.

13 Express your likes and dislikes about the political and social views of Prince Klemens von Metternich.

The Age of Democratic Revolution

The Execution of King Charles I

In England, a dramatic moment in history occurred when a bitter civil war erupted in the 1640s. The country was split into two forces called the Cavaliers and Roundheads. King Charles I made some unwise decisions and pushed the nation into civil war by refusing to acknowledge that Parliament had the right to pass laws in England. The collection of taxes and the right for Parliament to assemble on a regular basis were made into central issues.

Charles closed down the Parliament because he believed that God had made him king and he had the authority to rule England as he saw fit. The Cavaliers or supporters of the king, tended to be from the House of Lords and were Catholic. The Roundheads tended to be Puritans and from the House of Commons. They were led by Oliver Cromwell. Eventually, the Cavaliers were defeated, and King Charles was brought to trial and beheaded. Oliver Cromwell then governed the nation.

NEWS

Instructions: Write a newspaper article as if you were a reporter covering the trial and the execution of King Charles I.

10.2 Blackline Master • Visual/Spatial Activity

The Age of Democratic Revolution

The Guillotine and the Terror

In France, violent revolution broke out in 1789 against King Louis XVI. The nation suffered from political, social, and economic hardships. The country was on the verge of starvation due to recent crop failures. In addition to famine, the country was broke due to an unfair tax system. The First and Second Estates, made up of nobles and aristocrats, paid no tax while the Third Estate was taxed beyond reason.

On July 14, a mob attacked the Bastille, a prison in France. Rumor was that King Louis had his political opponents locked in the Bastille. The attack on this prison was the first violent act against the king.

Louis and his family later tried to flee France, but they were captured and returned to Paris. The king was now a prisoner and was branded a traitor. He was brought to trial and sent to the guillotine in 1793. A few weeks later, Marie Antoinette, wife of Louis, was also executed.

This was only the beginning; a massive bloodbath would follow. Led by Robespierre, a staunch opponent of King Louis, France would now enter a brief, horrifying period known as the Reign of Terror.

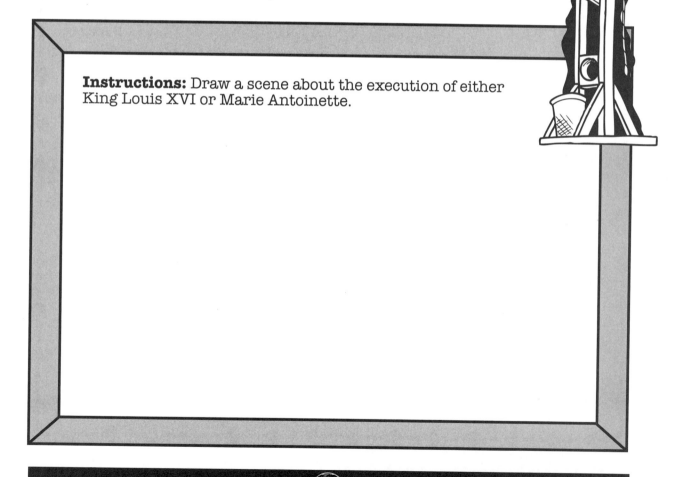

Instructions: Draw a scene about the execution of either King Louis XVI or Marie Antoinette.

Adventures Through World History! • Rickey Millwood
Kagan Publishing • 1 (800) 933-2667 • www.KaganOnline.com

10.3 Blackline Master • Intrapersonal Activity

The Age of Democratic Revolution

The Rise of a Dictator

In 1799, Napoléon Bonaparte would come to power through a coup d'etat. He took over the government of France by use of his military. Napoléon overthrew the Directory, which had not been able to rule France effectively after the execution of Robespierre. Napoléon had the ability to arouse French patriotism at a low point in their history. He captured the hearts and minds of his people.

Napoléon ruled France as a military dictator, but brought about many reforms. He opened the churches that Robespierre had closed, and he also opened the University of France. Nevertheless, he was a dictator and kept a close eye on his opponents, ruthlessly suppressing all political opposition. He demanded loyalty from the French people and set about to dominate Europe.

Napoléon

Instructions: In an essay, express your likes and dislikes about the rule of Napoléon Bonaparte. Collect ideas below.

Likes	Dislikes

10.4 Blackline Master • Naturalist Activity

The Age of Democratic Revolution

A Winter in Russia

There were two enemy nations in Europe that Napoléon was never able to conquer. These were England and Russia. His Continental System, a ploy to ruin England's trade, failed as did his major invasion of Russia. The catastrophe in Russia cost him nearly one-half million men. Only a handful of brave men straggled out of this campaign.

It has been said that the Russian winter defeated Napoléon rather than the Russian army. He would later be defeated for the last time at Waterloo, but the Russian invasion broke Napoléon's spirit and his army.

Instructions: Write about how the elements of a Russian winter cost Napoléon Bonaparte his Grand Army. Read your writing to a partner.

___

frozen rivers • snowdrifts • howling winds • icy roads • extreme temperatures

Adventures Through World History! • Rickey Millwood
Kagan Publishing • 1 (800) 933-2667 • www.KaganOnline.com

Chapter 11: The Industrial Revolution (1700–1900)

The Industrial Revolution (factory system) developed in England. England provided the resources and materials necessary for industrial development that would spread across Europe and to the world. The textile or clothing industry came first. The woolen industry would give way to the production of cotton garments.

England had an abundance of workers desperate for labor, and England had its colonies as customers for finished products. England had rivers for waterpower and harbors for shipping. England also had capital available for investments. All the ingredients were in place for industrialization.

Verbal/Linguistic

1 Read *Hard Times* by Charles Dickens.

2 Explain the concept "domestic system."

3 Explain the phrase "workshop of the world."

4 Read about the textile contributions of Richard Arkwright.

5 Write a paper about the working conditions in the textile mills.

6 Read poems about child labor in the textile mills.

7 Write a newspaper article about accidents in the industrial factories.

8 Share ideas about the importance of the steam engine to industrial development.

9 Explain why factory owners preferred to employ women and children.

10 Write a play or skit about life in an English industrial town.

11 Share ideas about the importance of the American South to the cotton industry of England.

12 Do a descriptive writing exercise about child labor in England's coal mine industry.

Logical/Mathematical

1 Brainstorm ideas that analyze why the Industrial Revolution began in England.

2 Create a ladder graphic organizer that illustrates the progression of various fields of industry in England.

3 Categorize the raw materials in England needed for industrial development.

4 Sequence the major inventions in the textile industry.

5 Create a graph illustrating a massive migration of farm workers to the English manufacturing centers.

6 Make predictions about the problems caused by rapid industrialization.

7 Discover patterns in canal building through England.

8 Determine the percentage of children employed in England from 1700–1900.

9 Evaluate the ideas that determine a nation's prosperity according to Adam Smith.

10 Relate the theories of overpopulation to poverty according to Thomas Malthus.

Adventures Through World History! • Rickey Millwood

Visual/Spatial

1 Examine political cartoons of child labor in the textile industry.

2 Paint or draw a scene of an industrial town.

3 Examine pictures of European clothing from the 1800s.

4 Examine pictures painted by Vincent van Gogh.

5 Examine the artwork of Paul Cézanne.

6 Create a picture of life during the Industrial Revolution in the style of the Impressionists.

7 Create a PowerPoint of the major textile inventions of the Industrial Revolution.

8 Create a PowerPoint of the development of the locomotive industry in England.

9 Design a postage stamp illustrating a medical breakthrough during the period 1700–1900.

10 Examine the photographs of Lewis Hine exposing child labor in America.

Musical/Rhythmic

1 Read about Henry Steinway and his pianos.

2 Learn about how the Industrial Revolution improved the quality of the sound of the piano.

3 Write a rap song about children being employed in the coal mine industry.

4 Listen to the music of Ludwig van Beethoven.

5 Listen to the music of Franz Haydn.

6 Listen to the music of Wolfgang Amadeus Mozart.

7 Learn about a particular instrument invented during the Industrial Revolution.

8 Learn about the improvement of instruments such as the bending of French horns into a coil.

9 Determine the role of horns in military battles during the 19th century.

10 Write a song about an inventor during the Industrial Revolution.

Adventures Through World History! • Rickey Millwood
Kagan Publishing • 1 (800) 933-2667 • www.KaganOnline.com

Chapter 11 continued
The Industrial Revolution (1700–1900)

Bodily/Kinesthetic

1 Perform a skit about child labor in an industrial European town.

2 Build a model of a cotton gin.

3 Examine cotton bolls.

4 Role-play Louis Pasteur explaining the importance of his medical research.

5 Role-play an Impressionist artist describing his or her style of painting.

6 Role-play the economist Thomas Malthus.

7 Perform a pantomime about a famous inventor during the Industrial Revolution.

8 Conduct an interview with a person that has been employed in the textile or garment industry.

9 Act out the role of an inventor threatened by the Luddites.

Naturalist

1 Record the stages in canal building in England to improve the nation's transportation system.

2 Examine cotton and feel the texture of the fabric.

3 Record the various types of minerals needed in the puddling process to produce iron.

4 Determine how the forests of England were affected by the Industrial Revolution.

5 Determine how industrial towns were affected by the burning of coal.

6 Record the changes in health problems of workers that breathed cotton dust.

7 Compare and contrast the coal mining industry of England with the coal mining industry of the United States.

8 Categorize the tools used by children in the coal mines of England.

9 Visit a museum that displays manufacturing artifacts from the 19th century.

10 Read about the work of Edward Jenner and smallpox vaccinations.

Adventures Through World History! • Rickey Millwood
Kagan Publishing • 1 (800) 933-2667 • www.KaganOnline.com

Interpersonal

1 Compare and contrast the domestic system with the factory system of England.

2 Discuss with a partner why the Industrial Revolution began in England.

3 Do a team presentation on the impact of the Enclosure Acts in England.

4 Role-play a child forced to work in the textile industry of England.

5 Solve problems that the rapid growth of industrialization caused in England.

6 Role-play a Luddite arrested for vandalizing machinery.

7 Interview other classmates about the coal mining industry of England.

8 Discuss how the works of Charles Dickens relate to the Age of Industrialization.

9 Reach a consensus explaining why the Industrial Revolution began in England before it did in America.

10 Share with the class information about the ideas of Karl Marx.

Intrapersonal

1 Describe your feelings about the major reasons why the Industrial Revolution began in England.

2 Write a poem about child labor in England.

3 Choose between the alternative of working in the textile or coal mine industry as a child.

4 Write a sanitation and pollution code to improve the quality of life in industrial towns.

5 Weigh alternatives to the pollution of the environment in industrial towns.

6 Defend the position that the steam engine was the most important invention during the Industrial Revolution.

7 Make a journal entry as if you were an inventor of the Industrial Revolution.

8 Defend or condemn the decision to execute Luddites for vandalizing industrial factories.

9 Write about the needs of the Luddites.

10 Prioritize materials needed for the development of the iron industry.

11 Read silently and reflect upon the works of Charles Dickens.

The Industrial Revolution

The Growth of Industry

England had the required elements necessary for industrial growth. Large mineral deposits, a large labor force, good ports for shipping, and a host of colonies for customers provided this island nation with just the right ingredients for industrialization.

There was an overabundance of workers who had been driven to the cities by the Enclosure Acts. Certainly there was never a shortage of labor. People were often desperate to accept any job. Jobs that we define as degrading, would be precious to a worker desperate for a job.

The first factories were the textile plants. These buildings generally were located on rivers for waterpower. England purchased cotton from its colonies and finished products were manufactured in England to be distributed globally. England was given the name "Workshop of the World."

HELP WANTED

Instructions: Create the name of a company. Then write an advertisement, to appear in the help wanted section of the paper for either textile mill workers or coal miners.

Company Name: _____

The Industrial Revolution

Life in Industrial Towns

Towns and workers faced numerous problems due to rapid industrial growth. During the Industrial Revolution, workers swarmed into these towns in search of employment. The towns were not equipped to handle this massive migration.

Workers faced dangerous machines and cruel supervisors on a daily basis. There was no minimum wage, and a typical day was 14 or more hours. The factories were crammed with small children; many of these children were severely injured or killed in industrial accidents.

It's difficult for us to imagine such horrifying working conditions. However, people in developing nations today face the same types of problems.

Instructions: Do a descriptive writing activity addressing both the factory and social evils that workers endured daily during the Industrial Revolution. Begin by recording some ideas below.

Factory Evils

_____
_____
_____
_____
_____
_____

Social Evils

_____
_____
_____
_____
_____
_____
_____

The Industrial Revolution

The Evils of Child Labor

Child labor was widely accepted during the Industrial Revolution. The prevailing thought was that hard work was good for the body and soul. It was also believed that these children had mouths and had to earn their own food.

The jobs were tedious and took their toll on children. They were deprived of an education and endured tormenting conditions in factories. They were chained to machines and physically abused by factory mangers for not working quickly or hard enough.

Factory owners desired children to work in their companies because they could pay them low wages. Children were passive and could be easily managed. Parents sent their children to work in these places because they were desperate for income.

Instructions: Have members of the class role-play groups of children employed in the following industries:

1. Coal mines
2. Textile or cotton mills
3. Canneries
4. Timber industry
5. Fish or seafood packinghouse
6. Glass factory
7. Iron Factory

The Industrial Revolution

The Views of an Economist

The economist Thomas Malthus believed that industrial workers suffered because they lacked skills to find more desirable work. He concluded that workers who lack skills will make low wages and will be employed in some of the worst jobs. He also believed that poverty is caused by overpopulation and argued that disease and war had kept down the world's population.

The eradication of diseases and more nutritious foods caused the rapid growth of the world's population during the Industrial Revolution. This intensified the problems predicted by Malthus. The theories of Malthus are pessimistic: He predicted that famine, disease, low wages, and unemployment would result from overpopulation.

Activity Options

1. Write about the wants and needs of people in Third World nations today. Consider the economic, medical, and social problems that people face each day.

2. Form solutions to the problems written about by Thomas Malthus.

Chapter 12 Era of World War I (1914–1920)

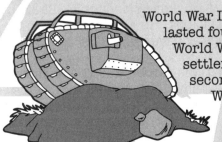

World War I, or the Great War, erupted in 1914. This bloody conflict lasted four brutal years and claimed over ten million lives.

World War I was said to be the war to "end all wars." In fact, the settlement of World War I planted the seeds for the coming of a second world war.

World War I started over a murder in the Balkans. However, underlying causes, such as imperialism and nationalism, set the stage for a world conflict. The United States remained neutral until 1917 when it entered the fray.

Verbal/Linguistic

1 Read *All Quiet on the Western Front*.

2 Share ideas about the background causes of World War I.

3 Explain the concept of unrestricted submarine warfare.

4 Do a creative writing exercise about the assassination of Archduke Ferdinand.

5 Write a poem about No Man's Land.

6 Keep a journal as if you were a soldier in the trenches of World War I.

7 Write a newspaper article about the sinking of the *Lusitania*.

8 Create a list of key vocabulary terms associated with World War I.

9 Discuss why Russia was defeated during World War I.

10 Explain why America entered World War I.

11 Debate the stipulations created in the Versailles Treaty.

12 Write a letter as a wife to her husband, an airplane pilot in World War I.

Logical/Mathematical

1 Analyze data about the loss of life in World War I.

2 Brainstorm ideas about the assassination of Archduke Ferdinand.

3 Sequence the events that led to the outbreak of World War I.

4 Calculate the probability of surviving the torpedo hit on the *Lusitania*.

5 Synthesize ideas about No Man's Land.

6 Classify the new weapons used in World War I.

7 Discover patterns in German submarine warfare.

8 Evaluate the reasons why America entered World War I in 1917.

9 Brainstorm ideas about the strategy of the Triple Entente.

10 Symbolize in numbers the loss of life from the major nations in World War I.

11 Solve the logistical problem of transporting American soldiers and supplies to the Western Front.

12 Analyze data about African American units that served in World War I.

Adventures Through World History! • Rickey Millwood
Kagan Publishing • 1 (800) 933-2667 • www.KaganOnline.com

Visual/Spatial

1 Create a political cartoon about the assassination of Archduke Ferdinand.

2 Create a political cartoon of European nations boasting their new weapons.

3 Watch the film *All Quiet on the Western Front*.

4 Watch the film *Paths of Glory*.

5 Draw a scene of No Man's Land.

6 Create a scene of the sinking of the *Lusitania*.

7 Create a newspaper article about America's entry into World War I.

8 Create a ladder graphic organizer that illustrates the causes that led America into World War I.

9 Create a PowerPoint of the various military uniforms worn in World War I.

10 Design a political cartoon about the Zimmermann Telegram.

11 Pretend you were a soldier that survived the trenches of World War I.

12 Imagine being one of the characters in *All Quiet on the Western Front*.

13 Visualize the scene aboard the *Lusitania* once it was hit by a torpedo.

14 Create a billboard advertising for young men to join the German army during World War I.

15 Draw a map of Europe at the conclusion of World War I.

Musical/Rhythmic

1 Listen to "*La Marseillaise*."

2 Listen to "Pack Up Your Troubles in an Old Kit Bag and Smile, Smile, Smile."

3 Listen to "Over There."

4 Listen to "We're All Going Calling on the Kaiser."

5 Listen to "Rule, Britannia!"

6 Listen to "It's a Long Way to Tipperary."

7 Evaluate the music from the era of World War I.

8 Write a song about a major event during World War I to the tune of a familiar song.

9 Create a rap song about a famous historical character from World War I.

10 Write a jingle advertising a new product from the era of World War I.

11 Play a song from World War I on an instrument before the class.

12 In groups, perform songs from the era of World War I.

Adventures Through World History! • Rickey Millwood

Chapter 12 continued
Era of World War I
(1914—1920)

Bodily/Kinesthetic

1 Act out the role of a European citizen after the outbreak of World War I.

2 Act out the role of American citizens in 1914 when World War I first erupted.

3 Perform a skit about young soldiers in Europe that have just been conscripted.

4 Visit World War I battlefields on the Internet.

5 Perform a skit about soldiers in the trenches of World War I.

6 Role-play a survivor from the *Lusitania*.

7 Read about the effects of chemical weapons on the soldiers in the trenches.

8 Act out the role of a famous aviator from World War I.

9 Perform a skit about the leaders of the major participants in World War I.

10 Visit a World War I memorial.

11 Role-play the Big Four at the Paris Peace Conference.

12 Design a computer game about the major events of World War I.

Naturalist

1 Determine the depth of the ocean where the *Lusitania* sank.

2 Determine the temperature of the ocean where the *Lusitania* sank.

3 List the characteristics of No Man's Land.

4 Record the changes in trench building from 1914 to 1918.

5 Examine pictures of the landscape on the battlefields of World War I.

6 Categorize the non-natural items found in the trenches.

7 List characteristics of the trenches.

8 Classify the materials used to construct submarines.

9 Classify the vegetables grown in America's victory gardens.

10 Classify the food items rationed during World War I in America.

11 Classify the nonperishable goods rationed in America during World War I.

12 Sort and categorize rationed items in the United States during World War I.

Interpersonal

1 Debate the impact that the Zimmermann Telegram had upon the United States.

2 Do a team presentation on the use of airplanes during World War I.

3 Interview other classmates about the causes of World War I.

4 Practice taking turns detailing how World War I affected women in Europe.

5 Share with others your thoughts about the new weapons used in World War I.

6 Practice compromising a solution (other than war) to the assassination of Archduke Ferdinand.

7 Reach a consensus on why World War I was so deadly.

8 Role-play soldiers that survived World War I.

9 Practice active listening as students describe the lessons learned from World War I.

10 Do a team presentation on how the map of Europe changed at the conclusion of World War I.

11 Practice criticizing European nations for allowing World War I to linger four bitter years.

12 Practice taking turns explaining how music impacted the morale of nations involved in World War I.

Intrapersonal

1 Defend the position by Austria to declare war in 1914.

2 Take a stance for America's neutrality in 1914.

3 Create an action plan that would have prevented the outbreak of World War I.

4 Describe your feelings about the sinking of the *Lusitania*.

5 Describe your feelings about the Sussex Pledge.

6 Observe the mood changes in French, German, and Russian soldiers by 1916.

7 Meditate on the actual causes that brought the United States into World War I.

8 Write a code of ethical conduct on the use of poison gas during World War I.

9 Describe your feelings about the use of the airplane in World War I.

10 Weigh alternatives to settlement of World War I rather than through the Versailles Treaty.

11 Write a personal poem about No Man's Land.

12 List the priorities of the major world leaders during World War I.

Era of World War I

The Sinking of the *Lusitania*

In May 1915, a terrible incident occurred at sea that had a great impact upon World War I. The Germans used a submarine to torpedo and sink a cruise ship called the *Lusitania*. The German high command had issued an order that ships in the war zone would be torpedoed. The *Lusitania* had departed from New York City and was within just a few miles of Ireland when the ship was destroyed. There were two explosions on the ship. The first explosion was a direct result of a strike by a torpedo. The second explosion remains a mystery. The Germans claimed to have launched only one torpedo; the British claimed the Germans launched two torpedoes. One thought is the second explosion took place because the ship was carrying war materials. Nevertheless, nearly 1,200 people were killed.

The American public was outraged over this incident; however, America did not enter World War I until 1917.

Instructions: Compare and contrast the sinking of the *Titanic* with the sinking of the *Lusitania*.

Titanic	*Lusitania*
Sequence the events that led to the sinking of both ships	
Water temperature	
Loss of life	
Time that elapsed before the vessel sank after being struck	
Political repercussions	

Adventures Through World History! • Rickey Millwood
Kagan Publishing • 1 (800) 933-2667 • www.KaganOnline.com

Era of World War I

Crossing No Man's Land

No Man's Land was the name given to the blood-soaked area between the opposing trenches. Terrible battles raged from 1914 until 1918, and millions died in the area called No Man's Land.

What kind of place was this region? This was an area littered with decomposing bodies and craters. It was an area that was referred to as a moonscape. This region was a lifeless place that soldiers repeatedly were forced to cross.

Sometimes as many as 50,000 men would fall in a single battle. The new machine gun mowed down thousands of young men as they surged out of their trench and headed toward enemy positions. Soldiers also faced poison gas. Today, the odor of death can still be detected on some of these battlefields.

Activity Options

1. Make a journal entry as if you were a young soldier about to cross No Man's Land.

2. Describe your feelings about World War I generals receiving promotions, based upon the amount of territory they could capture from the enemy, regardless of the loss of life.

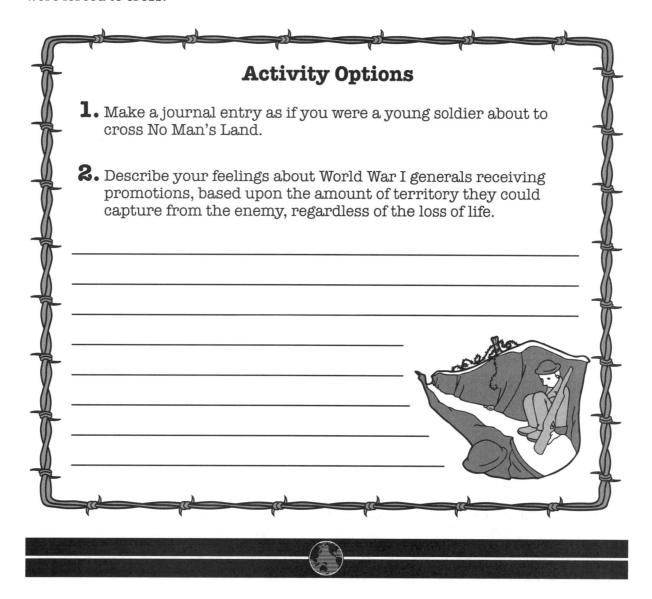

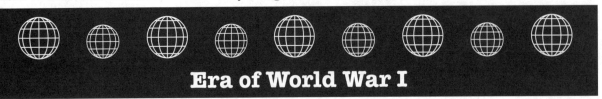

Era of World War I

America's Entry into World War I

There were several major factors that pulled the United States into World War I. Americans were furious at Germany because of the practice of unrestricted submarine warfare. (The United States had almost entered World War I over the sinking of the *Lusitania*).

President Wilson certainly demonstrated tremendous patience with Germany and was even elected in 1916 because he had kept America out of World War I. However, America's patience was wearing thin as the war lingered. Americans still viewed Germany as a nation with no respect for international law.

Later, a plot by Germany to involve Mexico in a war against America was uncovered. This plot was revealed in the Zimmermann Telegram. Germany supposedly promised four American states in the Southwest to Mexico if America was defeated in World War I.

America felt much sympathy toward the democracies of Britain and France. In 1917, America entered the conflict against Germany. President Wilson would now face the daunting task of preparing a nation for entry into this horrific event.

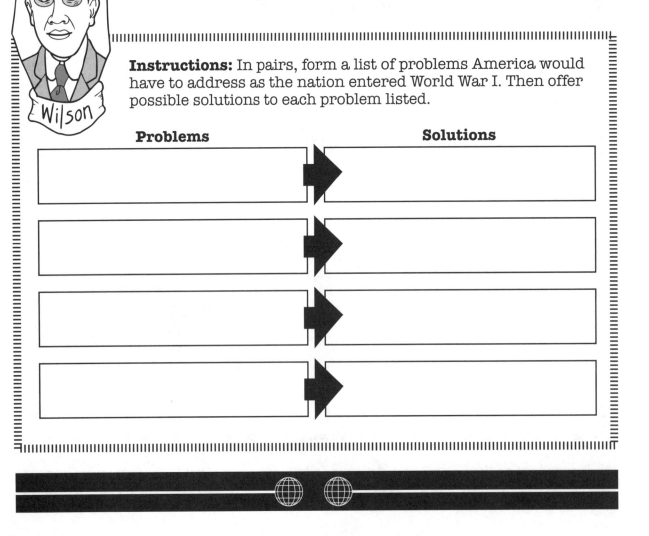

Instructions: In pairs, form a list of problems America would have to address as the nation entered World War I. Then offer possible solutions to each problem listed.

Problems	Solutions

12.4 Blackline Master • Logical/Mathematical Activity

Era of World War I

Misconceptions about World War I

In 1914, it would have been hard to convince anyone that the war would last four years and ten million people would die. Yet, that is exactly what happened.

What were some of the misconceptions about the war in 1914? First, most people thought the war would be settled after a few big battles. Some soldiers even believed that they would be home by Christmas. Some people thought the war would be a great adventure and readily volunteered to fight. Most people thought the loss of life would be small and the war would be short.

The actual truth was very different. The new weapons provided tremendous killing power; the trenches became massive graveyards. The war certainly turned out much differently in 1918 than had been earlier anticipated.

Instructions: Compare misconceptions about World War I with America's current involvement in Iraq.

WW1	Iraq

Chapter 13: The Rise of Dictators (1919–1939)

The period between the two World Wars is known as the Rise of Dictators. Vladimir Lenin came to power in Russia and initiated a form of government called Communism. Benito Mussolini and Adolf Hitler came to power in Italy and Germany; these men introduced the World to Fascism and Nazism. How did these individuals come to power and how did they impact history? Why did the people of Europe turn their nations over to these tyrants? These dictators would shape Europe's history for decades to come.

Verbal/Linguistic

1 Share ideas detailing how the Communist party came to power in Russia.

2 Compare and contrast Communism and Nazism.

3 Discuss how Lenin was able to gain control of Russia in November 1917.

4 Do a creative writing exercise about life in Italy under the dictatorship of Benito Mussolini.

5 Discuss the economic conditions in Germany in 1932.

6 Do a descriptive writing exercise about the early life of Adolf Hitler.

7 Do selective readings from *The Rise and Fall of the Third Reich*.

8 Write a newspaper article about the 1932 presidential election in Germany.

9 Write a paper describing the Reichstag fire in Germany.

10 Write a research paper on the Gestapo.

11 Conduct read-alouds from passages of *Mein Kampf*.

12 Listen to a speech by Adolf Hitler and discuss why he was an effective speaker.

Logical/Mathematical

1 Sequence the events that led to the overthrow of the Russian government by the Bolsheviks.

2 Analyze data about the number of deaths during the Russian Civil War.

3 Organize a list of changes in Russia after Lenin came to power and executed Czar Nicholas II.

4 Explain why Benito Mussolini and Adolf Hitler formed a partnership.

5 Examine the unemployment rate in Germany in 1932.

6 Discover trends in Adolf Hitler's military moves.

7 Organize facts describing how the Jews were treated in Germany from 1933 to 1945.

8 Analyze data about the 1932 presidential election in Germany.

9 Make associations between the Fascists and Nazis.

10 Analyze why the United States did not prevent Adolf Hitler from coming to power.

Visual/Spatial

1 Examine political cartoons of Adolf Hitler and Benito Mussolini.

2 Examine the propaganda symbols and slogans used by the Nazi party.

3 Watch the film *The Rise and Fall of the Third Reich*.

4 Examine pictures of the various uniforms worn by the Nazis.

5 Draw a scene depicting the impact that the Great Depression had on Germany.

6 Watch a film about Vladimir Lenin's rise to power.

7 Create a graphic organizer that illustrates Stalin's rise to power in the Soviet Union.

8 Watch a film about the life of Josef Stalin.

9 Watch the film *Triumph of the Will*.

10 Create a drawing about the 1936 Olympics in Germany.

11 Draw a scene about Jesse Owens in the 1936 Olympics.

12 Make a poster illustrating how Germany changed during the Third Reich.

13 Create a map of Germany and label the major concentration camps.

14 Watch the film *The Twisted Cross*.

15 Examine the painting *Guernica* by Pablo Picasso.

Musical/Rhythmic

1 Listen to the music of Richard Wagner.

2 Evaluate the music heard in Germany under the Nazis.

3 Write a song about a European dictator.

4 Write a song about a major event in Europe between 1919 and 1939.

5 Write a poem about the goals of the Nazi party.

6 Listen to the music of gypsies from Romania.

7 Interpret the lyrics to any song played during the Russian Revolution.

8 Evaluate the music heard in Russia after the Communist takeover.

9 Determine how songs and parades played a role in the rise of the Nazi party.

10 Write a jingle about a new consumer product in the 1930s.

11 Create a song about Albert Einstein.

Adventures Through World History! • Rickey Millwood

Chapter 13 continued
The Rise of Dictators
(1919–1939)

Bodily/Kinesthetic

1 Act out the role of Jesse Owens at the 1936 Olympics.

2 Write a story as if you were a reporter covering the 1936 Olympics.

3 Create a skit about life in Russia after Lenin came to power.

4 Examine film of the Brown Shirts marching through the streets of Germany.

5 Visit a concentration camp in Germany on the Internet.

6 Perform a skit about the Munich Conference.

7 Act out the role of a Jewish citizen in Germany after the Nuremberg Laws were passed.

8 Conduct research to determine the cause of the death of Vladimir Lenin.

9 Build a model of the Kremlin.

10 Perform a skit about the Five-Year Plans under Josef Stalin.

Naturalist

1 Record the changes in agricultural production in Russia after the Communists came to power.

2 Describe the topography of the Rhineland.

3 List the characteristics of the Ruhr Valley.

4 Record the changes in industrial production in Germany after 1933.

5 Describe the physical characteristics of a concentration camp in Germany.

6 Record the developmental changes in the French Maginot Line.

7 Identify the resources in Ethiopia coveted by Fascist Italy.

8 Categorize the materials used as weapons by the Ethiopians against Italy in 1936.

9 Research the types of diseases that were common in the concentration camps.

Interpersonal

1 Discuss with a classmate the policies of the Nazi party.

2 Do a team presentation on a dictator that came to power in Europe during the 1920s or 1930s.

3 Share with others your thoughts about how the Communists came to power in Russia.

4 Reach a consensus explaining how the Great Depression led to the rise of the Nazi party.

5 Share with others how life changed in Germany during the Third Reich.

6 Role-play Jewish citizens living in Germany in 1936.

7 Interview each other about the implications of the Versailles Treaty.

8 Discuss with a partner the impact of the Reichstag fire.

9 Share with others your thoughts on the Italian invasion of Ethiopia.

10 Make a team project about the Rome-Berlin Axis agreement.

11 Write a collaborative paper about life in the Soviet Union under Josef Stalin.

12 Discuss with a classmate the goals that Hitler wrote in *Mein Kampf*.

13 Conduct an interview with any soldier that served in World War II.

Intrapersonal

1 Make an action plan that would have prevented Adolf Hitler's rise to power.

2 Make a journal entry as if you were a Jewish citizen living in Germany in 1933.

3 Observe the mood changes in Germans as they listen to Hitler's speeches.

4 Prioritize the goals of the Nazis once they were in power.

5 Describe your feelings about the Communist takeover in Russia.

6 Describe your feelings about how the Great Depression contributed to the cause of World War II.

7 Describe your feelings about America's policy of neutrality when World War II erupted.

8 Think about the actions of the British and French just before World War II started.

9 Defend or criticize the position by the United States to restrict immigration during the 1930s.

10 Express your likes and dislikes about the Versailles Treaty.

11 Write about the invasion of the neutral Rhineland by German troops.

12 Write about the actions of Neville Chamberlain after Germany invaded Poland in 1939.

13 Write about the painting *Guernica* by Pablo Picasso.

14 Meditate on the thought that the seeds of hatred and revenge were planted at the end of World War I and caused World War II.

15 Defend the position by Josef Stalin to industrialize the Soviet Union in the 1930s.

Adventures Through World History!

The Rise of Dictators

Repercussions from Versailles

In 1919, the Versailles Treaty was designed to settle World War I with Germany. A major mistake was made by not allowing Germany to have any say in the treaty stipulations.

The Big Four that designed the treaty did not make a lasting peace with Germany.

Germany was blamed in the treaty for World War I and humiliated by the treaty's many stipulations. The treaty planted the seeds of hatred that Hitler would use to incite the German people to begin another World War.

Instructions: Research the clauses in the Versailles Treaty that punished and humiliated Germany. Then, create a treaty that you feel would have been a fair settlement to World War I.

13.2 Blackline Master • Interpersonal Activity

The Rise of Dictators

The 1936 Olympics

In 1936 the Olympics were held in Berlin, Germany. The games would not be played again until 1944 because of World War II. Adolf Hitler took advantage of the 1936 games to show off his Nazi propaganda.

These games will forever be remembered because of the African American track star, Jesse Owens. Owens won three gold metals, which infuriated Adolf Hitler. More recently, Olympic events have also been marked by political events.

Instructions: Do a team presentation on how the following Olympic events have been affected by political acts or terrorism.

- 1972 Munich Games
- 1980 Moscow Games
- 1984 Los Angeles Games
- 1996 Atlanta Games

Adventures Through World History! • Rickey Millwood
Kagan Publishing • 1 (800) 933-2667 • www.KaganOnline.com

13.3 Blackline Master • Logical/Mathematical Activity

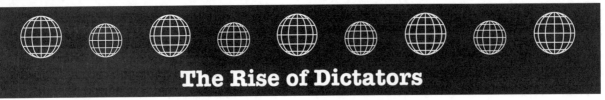

The Rise of Dictators

The Impact of the Great Depression

The Great Depression was another contributing factor that led to World War II. The Depression started in America but quickly spread around the world. European nations were devastated by the Depression.

Hard economic times often lead people into believing that strong men or demagogues can solve their problems. Benito Mussolini and Adolf Hitler both used the Depression to their advantage. Hitler, a fiery speaker, captivated the German population. The dictators promised food and jobs to the hungry masses.

Unfortunately, the people of these two nations were to suffer tremendously in the decades that followed. It would take World War II to free the people from these diabolical men.

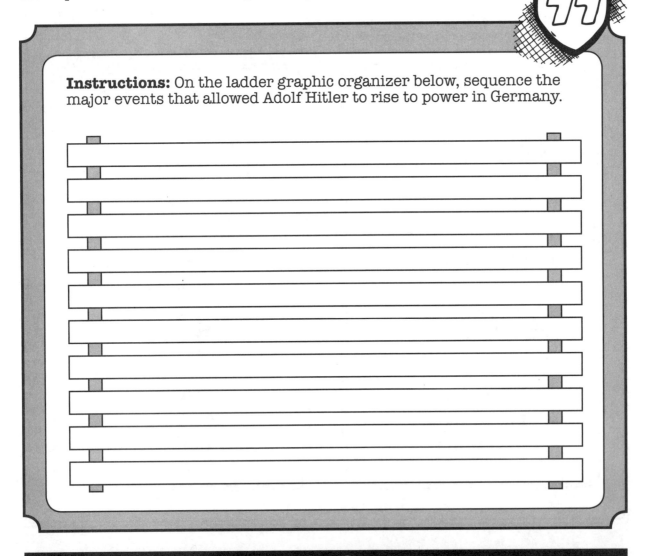

Instructions: On the ladder graphic organizer below, sequence the major events that allowed Adolf Hitler to rise to power in Germany.

Adventures Through World History! • Rickey Millwood
Kagan Publishing • 1 (800) 933-2667 • www.KaganOnline.com

13.4 Blackline Master • Visual/Spatial Activity

The Rise of Dictators

The Bolsheviks Gain Power

In 1917, the Bolsheviks, or Communists, came to power in Russia. The Bolsheviks were led by Vladimir Lenin who had promised the Russian people, "Peace, Land, and Bread." Lenin took Russia out of World War I but a bloody civil war erupted between the "Reds" and "Whites." Eventually, Lenin and the "Reds" won this war. Lenin then began to transform Russia into the Communist state he desired.

Life drastically changed in Russia after the Communists came to power. The people lost individual rights, and the economy was controlled by the state. Churches were closed. The Communists ruled by brutality and terror.

Russia, which became part of the Soviet Union, would remain Communist until the nation fragmented in 1990. In 1924, Lenin died of a stroke but would be followed by history's most notorious dictator, Josef Stalin.

Instructions: Create a political cartoon that shows how life changed in Russia once the Communists seized power.

Adventures Through World History! • Rickey Millwood

Chapter 14

The Holocaust
(1933–1945)

In 1933, Adolf Hitler came to power in Germany. He had been appointed Chancellor by President Paul von Hindenburg. When Hindenburg died, Hitler quickly combined the offices of Chancellor and the Presidency. Hitler was now in full control of Germany and would be known as *der Führer* or the leader. By the mid-1930s, Hitler passed a series of laws aimed at the Jews. These were the Numemberg Laws, which were intended to punish and harass the Jews in Germany. In November 1938, open warfare against the Jews erupted in what was called the Kristallnacht or the "Night of the Broken Glass." Many believe this event was the start of the Holocaust. Many large concentration camps and killing centers would be opened in Germany and Poland to eradicate the people Hitler called "undesirable." Over ten million innocent victims would perish during the Holocaust. The world would be introduced to a new term called *genocide*.

Verbal/Linguistic

1 Read or conduct read-alouds from *The Diary of Anne Frank*, *Night*, or *Terrible Things: An Allegory of the Holocaust*.

2 Describe causes of the Holocaust.

3 Discuss how Hitler persuaded German companies to construct concentration camps and crematoriums.

4 Write a poem or give a speech as if you were a Holocaust survivor.

5 Compare and contrast the Holocaust with other historical events that involve genocide.

6 Write a research paper on a concentration camp or extermination camp.

7 Do a descriptive writing exercise about the food prisoners were fed in the camps.

8 Write a newspaper article about the Kristallnacht.

9 Write a letter as if you were a soldier that liberated a concentration camp.

10 Keep a journal as if you were in a concentration camp.

Logical/Mathematical

1 Calculate the probability of surviving in a concentration camp in Nazi Germany.

2 Analyze data about the ethnic backgrounds of concentration camp victims.

3 Brainstorm ideas about the deception of the concentration camps.

4 Conduct an experiment to determine the number of calories found in the food that was fed to prisoners in the concentration camps.

5 List and organize facts about the medical experiments performed in the concentration camps.

6 Compare and contrast any two concentration or extermination camps.

7 Formulate a hypothesis explaining why the Holocaust was allowed to take place.

8 Sequence the major events of the Holocaust beginning with the Kristallnacht.

9 Discover patterns in the construction of the concentration camps.

10 Synthesize ideas about the number of deaths in the extermination camps.

Visual/Spatial

1 Examine the artwork of David Olére.

2 Watch *Uprising*.

3 Watch the film *Escape From Sobibor*.

4 Watch the film *The Devil's Arithmetic*.

5 Watch any documentary on the Holocaust.

6 Examine pictures on the Internet of concentration camps or extermination camps.

7 Make a poster about the causes of the Holocaust.

8 Create a PowerPoint of the major events of the Holocaust.

9 Examine historical photographs of the concentration camps being liberated.

10 Pretend you were a Holocaust rescuer or survivor and draw a scene you witnessed in a concentration camp.

11 Imagine and detail the conditions people endured in the concentration camps.

12 Draw a train scene showing victims being transported to a concentration camp.

Musical/Rhythmic

1 Learn about music played for victims once they arrived at concentration camps.

2 Listen to the music played in Germany during the Holocaust.

3 Compose a melody about a particular concentration camp.

4 Learn about folk dances camp victims were forced to perform in the camps.

5 Listen to the music of different cultures of Europeans during the early 1940s.

6 Determine why the Nazis played music for camp victims as they were placed in the gas chambers.

7 Research information about any composers that died during the Holocaust.

8 Listen to and interpret the songs in the Warsaw Ghetto uprising.

9 Evaluate the music Americans were listening to during the Holocaust.

10 Write a song about a major event of the Holocaust.

Adventures Through World History! • Rickey Millwood
Kagan Publishing • 1 (800) 933-2667 • www.KaganOnline.com

Chapter 14 continued
The Holocaust (1933–1945)

Bodily/Kinesthetic

1 Role-play Holocaust survivors and tell your survival story before the class.

2 Visit a concentration camp in Germany or Poland on the Internet.

3 Visit any Holocaust museum in the United States.

4 Interview a Holocaust survivor.

5 Perform a skit about a family who escaped from Germany during the Holocaust.

6 Role-play American soldiers liberating concentration camps.

7 Role-play General Eisenhower giving a press conference about the atrocities discovered as the camps were opened.

8 Create the badges that Holocaust victims were forced to wear.

9 Role-play Corrie ten Boom after she was liberated from Ravensbrük.

Naturalist

1 List the physical characteristics of a concentration camp.

2 Record the developmental states of the concentration camps.

3 Describe the conditions on the trains that transported victims to the camps.

4 Discuss the experiments that took place in the camps that involved weather.

5 Classify the materials used to construct concentration camps.

6 Categorize the items removed from camp victims after they arrived.

7 Read about the Zyklon gas used in the gas chambers.

8 Research the symptoms of typhus.

9 Categorize the items destroyed on the Kristallnacht.

10 Create a display of any foods that were fed to camp victims.

11 Examine photos of the wooden beds in camp barracks where prisoners slept.

Adventures Through World History! • Rickey Millwood
Kagan Publishing • 1 (800) 933-2667 • www.KaganOnline.com

Interpersonal

1 Discuss with a classmate the root causes of the Holocaust.

2 Reach a consensus explaining why the Holocaust took place in a modern nation.

3 Do a team presentation on the concentration camps.

4 Interview classmates about the extermination camps in Poland.

5 Practice criticizing America for not intervening earlier to end the Holocaust.

6 Share with classmates your thoughts about the Holocaust.

7 Write a collaborative paper on one aspect of the Holocaust.

8 In teams of four, prepare news reports on a particular aspect of the Holocaust.

9 Share with others information that was intended to deceive camp victims once they arrived at a camp.

10 Interview each other about the Einsatzgruppen.

11 Practice taking turns recommending books to read about the Holocaust.

12 Re-create the Nuremberg Trials.

Intrapersonal

1 Form an action plan to escape from a concentration camp.

2 Describe your feelings about the conditions in the concentration camps.

3 Prioritize the needs of camp victims in order to stay alive.

4 Meditate about the toughest aspect of life in a concentration camp.

5 Make a journal entry as if you were a concentration camp victim.

6 Defend the position to let some concentration camps remain standing after the Holocaust ended.

7 Describe your feelings about the study of the Holocaust.

8 Write a personal poem about the Holocaust.

9 Respond to the hypothetical situation of living in Germany during the Holocaust.

10 Choose between the alternative of hiding someone from the SS or turning them away.

11 Write about the building of the Holocaust Museum in Washington DC.

12 Write about events in recent history much like the Holocaust.

13 Meditate on the reasons the Holocaust was allowed to happen.

14 Read *Terrible Things: An Allergy of the Holocaust* and write your opinion about this story.

14.1 Blackline Master • Verbal/Linguistic Activity

The Holocaust

The Kristallnacht

In November 1938, the Nazis launched a brutal and vicious attack all over Germany against the Jews. This event is known in history as the Kristallnacht or the "Night of the Broken Glass." Hitler's thugs smashed the windows of Jewish shops and torched Jewish synagogues. Jews were beaten in the streets, and their homes and shops were looted. The Jewish citizens were then billed for the cleanup of glass in the streets. Many historians consider this horrific event the beginning of the Holocaust.

Instructions: Imagine you were a Jew and just experienced the Night of the Broken Glass. Write a letter to your friend describing your experience and what to do about it.

Dear _____,

_____
_____
_____
_____
_____
_____
_____
_____
_____
_____
_____

Adventures Through World History! • Rickey Millwood
Kagan Publishing • 1 (800) 933-2667 • www.KaganOnline.com

14.2 Blackline Master • Visual/Spatial Activity

The Holocaust

A Glimpse into the Camps

The artwork of David Olère is very important to those studying the Holocaust. Olère was able to survive in the camps because of his art and ability to speak several languages. His art gives the viewer a glimpse of what really happened in the concentration and extermination camps.

After Olère was liberated, he dedicated his life to drawing scenes he witnessed or performed during the Holocaust. His art is important from a historical standpoint because it provides a form of visual documentation of the gruesome atrocities.

Instructions: Examine the Holocaust art of David Olère. Then, create a Holocaust art scene as if you were a Holocaust survivor telling your story though your illustration.

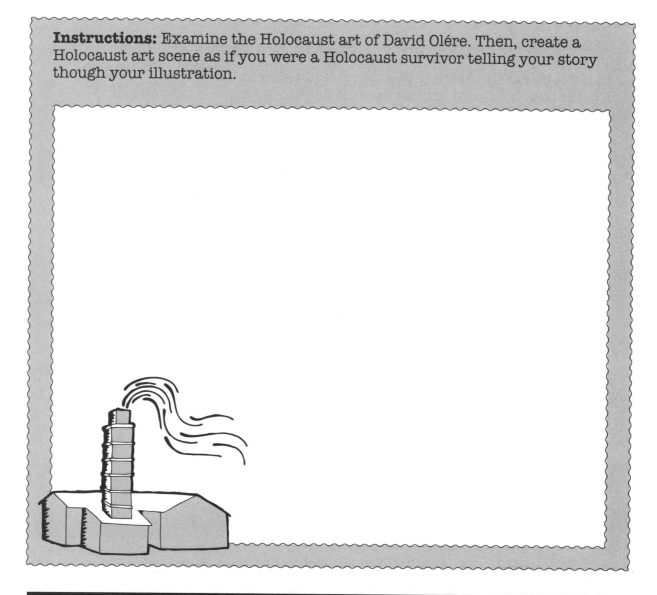

Adventures Through World History! • Rickey Millwood
Kagan Publishing • 1 (800) 933-2667 • www.KaganOnline.com

The Holocaust

Arrival at an Extermination

The concentration camps and extermination camps were often disguised, and guards deceived victims into believing that if they worked hard they would live. The words over the camp gate read, "Work makes one free". Guards told victims that they would be given medical care and could write letters to their loved ones back home. Victims were told that as long as they worked hard, they would be kept alive. The SS even disguised the gas chambers to look like showers. The guards sometimes played music to the new arrivals to soothe their fears. This was all done to prevent panic and disorder.

We must always remember that millions died in awful camps such as Auschwitz, Treblinka, and Belzec.

Instructions: In a team of four, write and perform a skit about a family that just arrived by train at a concentration or extermination camp.

Character 1	Character 2
Character 3	Character 4

14.4 Blackline Master • Intrapersonal Activity

The Holocaust

Monuments of the Holocaust

Many of the concentration and extermination camps were allowed to remain standing after World War II. Visitors may tour these facilities today and see these nightmarish places where the Holocaust occurred. These monuments represent the brutality that victims endured for nearly seven years until they were finally liberated.

Instructions: Do you feel the camps should remain standing or should be torn down? Explain your stance.

Adventures Through World History! • Rickey Millwood
Kagan Publishing • 1 (800) 933-2667 • www.KaganOnline.com

Chapter 15: World War II (1939–1945)

World War II erupted on September 1, 1939, with the German invasion of Poland. Germany had practiced earlier for World War II in Spain and was prepared to launch its devastating blitzkrieg attack. Hitler had perfected his tactics; Poland would be devastated in a matter of hours. The German air force, or Luftwaffe, was brutal as it obliterated the forces of Poland.

The world had never seen such a devastating war machine. Other nations would soon face the type of onslaught the Poles encountered. It would take six bitter years to bring World War II to an end.

Verbal/Linguistic

1 Compare and contrast the tactics of World War I and World War II.

2 Do a descriptive writing exercise about blitzkrieg tactics.

3 Debate the Hitler-Stalin Pact.

4 Explain why the French Maginot Line failed.

5 Give a speech that Winston Churchill gave about Britain's war against Germany.

6 Do a creative writing exercise about the Battle of Britain.

7 Write a newspaper article about the Japanese attack on Pearl Harbor.

8 Write a play about the attack on Pearl Harbor.

9 Read about Operation Barbarossa.

10 Explain the concept of "total war."

11 Write a book report on a famous general during World War II.

12 Share ideas explaining why America did not enter World War II until 1941.

Logical/Mathematical

1 Analyze data about the total number of deaths during World War II.

2 Determine the cost in dollars of World War II.

3 Create a time line of the major battles of World War II.

4 Brainstorm ideas about Hitler's strategy during World War II.

5 Discover trends in the German occupation of nations they conquered.

6 Organize facts about the Battle of Britain.

7 Compare and contrast the British Royal Air Force and the mighty German Luftwaffe.

8 Organize facts about the Einsatzgruppen or special death squads.

9 Compare and contrast the invasion of Russia by Napoléon Bonaparte with the invasion of Russia by Adolf Hitler.

10 Sequence the events on D-Day.

11 Use deductive reasoning to determine why the July Plot of 1944 failed.

12 List the reasons why Germany, Italy, and Japan lost World War II.

Visual/Spatial

1 Draw a scene of the German invasion of Poland.

2 Watch the film *The Battle of Britain*.

3 Watch the film *Pearl Harbor*.

4 Watch the film *Tora! Tora! Tora!*

5 Watch the film *Midway*.

6 Watch the film *Sands of Iwo Jima*.

7 Create a flier urging young Americans to volunteer for the Army after Pearl Harbor.

8 Design a postcard about World War II.

9 Draw a scene about the Battle of Stalingrad.

10 Examine pictures of the uniforms worn during World War II.

11 View pictures on the Internet of the atomic bombs dropped on Japan.

12 Examine pictures of Hiroshima and Nagasaki after they were destroyed by atomic warfare.

Musical/Rhythmic

1 Evaluate patriotic music played in America during World War II.

2 Write a song about a major event during World War II.

3 Listen to the music of Woody Guthrie.

4 Listen to the song "Cowards Over Pearl Harbor."

5 Listen to the song "We're Gonna Hang Out the Washing On the Siegfried Line."

6 Listen to the song *Boogie Woogie Bugle Boy*.

7 Listen to the song "In the Füehrer's Face."

8 Write a jingle about a new consumer product sold during World War II.

9 Write a report on a famous musician during World War II.

10 Learn about the music that Adolf Hitler enjoyed.

11 Perform a famous dance during the era of World War II.

12 Play songs before the class on instruments from the World War II era.

Adventures Through World History! • Rickey Millwood
Kagan Publishing • 1 (800) 933-2667 • www.KaganOnline.com

Chapter 15 continued
World War II
(1939–1945)

Bodily/Kinesthetic

1 Act out the role of Josef Stalin after he learned that Germany had invaded the Soviet Union.

2 Act out the role of President Roosevelt after hearing the news of Pearl Harbor.

3 Build a model of a World War II battleship or aircraft carrier.

4 Visit the American Air and Space Museum in Washington DC.

5 Perform a popular dance from the era of World War II.

6 Perform a skit about the decision to drop two atomic bombs on Japan.

7 Create a crossword puzzle about World War II.

8 Visit a World War II battlefield on the Internet.

9 Interview a soldier that served in World War II.

10 Interview a person that remembers the attack on Pearl Harbor.

11 Role-play a scientist working on the Manhattan Project.

12 Role-play Albert Einstein during World War II.

Naturalist

1 Record the winter conditions in Russia that the German army faced in 1942.

2 List the symptoms of hypothermia.

3 Record the weather conditions on D-Day.

4 List the characteristics of the beaches where the Allies landed on D-Day.

5 Record the changes and impact of the weather during the Battle of the Bulge.

6 Examine photographs of atomic bomb tests in New Mexico.

7 Examine the conditions faced by German civilians during firestorm raids.

8 Read about the effect of the atomic bombs dropped on Hiroshima and Nagasaki.

9 Determine how the use of atomic bombs in Japan affected the environment.

10 Learn how the United States developed atomic weapons from uranium.

11 Examine photographs of Hiroshima and Nagasaki after the atomic bombs were dropped.

12 Watch the film *Sands of Iwo Jima* and examine the topography of the island.

13 Compare the effects of the Russian winter in World War II with the Russian winter that Napoléon faced.

Adventures Through World History! • Rickey Millwood
Kagan Publishing • 1 (800) 933-2667 • www.KaganOnline.com

Interpersonal

1 Discuss with a classmate the reasons why Adolf Hitler attacked Poland.

2 Do a team presentation on the French surrender to Germany in June 1940.

3 Interview each other about the Battle of Britain.

4 Share with classmates the importance of the Lend-Lease Act.

5 Role-play Winston Churchill during the Battle of Britain.

6 Discuss in a small group the tactics of the Einsatzgruppen.

7 Reach a consensus on the impact of the battle of Stalingrad.

8 Solve problems that the Russians faced during the German invasion of their country.

9 Debate the issue to invade Iwo Jima.

10 Discuss the decision to drop two atomic bombs on Japan.

11 With a partner, write a report on the kamikaze planes.

12 Role-play Franklin Roosevelt, Josef Stalin, and Winston Churchill at the Yalta Conference.

Intrapersonal

1 Describe your feelings about the Hitler-Stalin Pact.

2 Make an action plan the French could have employed to prevent a fast surrender to Germany.

3 Observe mood changes in Americans after Pearl Harbor was attacked.

4 Make a journal entry as if you were an American landing on Omaha Beach on D-Day.

5 Express your likes and dislikes about the rationing of products during World War II.

6 Defend the position to defeat Germany and Italy before Japan during World War II.

7 Think about the actions of the German generals during the July Plot.

8 Write an ethical code of conduct for the treatment of American prisoners captured by the Japanese.

9 Do you think military attacks on civilian targets are ever justified? Defend your position.

10 Think about the actions of soldiers as they liberated concentration camps.

11 Write about the efforts to capture Adolf Hitler by the Russians.

12 Think about the actions of President Truman as he decided to drop two atomic bombs on Japan.

13 Write a personal poem about a major event during World War II.

15.1 Blackline Master • Visual/Spatial Activity

World War II

Germany Practices for World War II

On April 26, 1937, the German Luftwaffe devastated the Spanish city of Guernica. Over 1,600 people died in this raid as Nazi Germany came to the assistance of Francisco Franco in Spain. The civil war in Spain was an opportunity for Germany to practice and prepare for World War II. Hitler used Guernica as a place to practice dive bombing tactics and to drive fear and horror into the hearts of civilians. The artist Pablo Picasso painted an abstract picture of the bombing of Guernica. This is one of his most famous paintings and gives a glimpse of the horror that would follow in World War II.

Instructions: Study the painting *Guernica* by Pablo Picasso. Then, create a scene from World War II in the style of Pablo Picasso.

Adventures Through World History! • Rickey Millwood
Kagan Publishing • 1 (800) 933-2667 • www.KaganOnline.com

World War II

Stalingrad—the Turning Point

On June 22, 1941, the German army invaded the Soviet Union. Hitler had broken the Hitler-Stalin Nonaggression Pact and set out to conquer the Soviet Union. Hitler coveted the oil and food reserves in the Soviet Union. He had written in his book *Mein Kampf* that the German people would live on the black soil of Russia. The German blitzkrieg advanced quickly in the Soviet Union but was halted by the Russian winter and tough resistance. Temperatures fell to -40 degrees and snow was waist-deep. The war bogged down all across the Soviet Union until the Germans were dealt a devastating blow at Stalingrad. The winter—and tough Russian resistance—played a major part in the German loss in the Soviet Union.

Instructions: How did the extreme Russian winter affect the outcome of World War II? Describe four effects of the winter.

1.
2.
3.
4.

The Attack at Pearl Harbor

On December 7, 1941, Japan launched a surprise air attack against the United States at Pearl Harbor, Hawaii. The United States suffered terrible losses to its battleships and land-based aircraft. Over 2,000 Americans died that somber day.

America was caught off guard and immediately declared war on Japan. The United States would now enter the war against the Axis nations. The Japanese had not told their war partner Hitler that they were going to attack the United States; Hitler was stunned to learn the news. Hitler was forced to declare war upon America. Soon his Third Reich would face not only the British and Russians, but also the Americans.

Instructions: Have students role-play the following scenarios:

World War II

The Atomic Bombs

On August 6 and August 9, 1945, the United States dropped two atomic bombs on Japan. These awesome weapons obliterated two Japanese cities in seconds. Buildings melted and thousands died instantly from the atomic blasts. Thousands would also die later as a result of radiation exposure.

Hiroshima and Nagasaki paid a heavy price when Japan defiantly refused to surrender to the United States. President Truman decided to use atomic weapons to bring the war to a quick end and save lives. The war did end immediately, but a new age followed. This would be the beginning of the atomic or nuclear age.

Instructions: Have students research and do presentations on the following:

- Manhattan Project
- Little Boy and Fat Man
- Paul Tibbets and Chuck Sweeney
- Enola Gay and Bock's Car
- Bombings of Hiroshima and Nagasaki

Chapter 16: The Cold War (1945–1991)

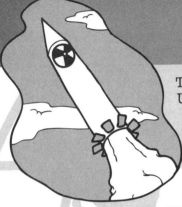

The partnership between Britain, the United States, and the Soviet Union quickly dissolved immediately after World War II. The Soviet Union broke the Yalta Agreement and gobbled up the nations of Eastern Europe. These nations became puppet or satellite nations to the Soviet Union. Winston Churchill proclaimed, "An iron curtain has descended across the continent." The United States and the Soviet Union competed around the world—militarily and economically—for the next five decades. There were several crucial episodes that nearly brought the two superpowers to nuclear war. The most serious event was the Cuban Missile Crisis in 1962. In 1990, the Soviet Union broke up and the Cold War came to an end.

Verbal/Linguistic

1 Discuss the decision by Josef Stalin to take over Eastern Europe after World War II.

2 Explain the phrase "Cold War."

3 Describe how Churchill's famous Iron Curtain speech contributed to the Cold War.

4 Write a play about a major Cold War event.

5 Compare and contrast the American and Soviet space programs.

6 Write a poem about the Sputnik satellite.

7 Write a newspaper article about the construction of the Berlin Wall.

8 Read about America's involvement in Korea and Vietnam.

9 Do a creative writing exercise about the Cuban Missile Crisis.

10 Explain the concept of containment.

11 Discuss the purpose of the Marshall Plan and Truman Doctrine.

12 Write about the Communist takeover in China in 1949.

Logical/Mathematical

1 Analyze data about the economic impact of the Marshall Plan.

2 Compare and contrast the Soviet and American military and nuclear buildup during the arms race.

3 Calculate the military strength of the NATO and Warsaw Pact nations during the Cold War.

4 Sequence 10 major events of the Cold War from 1945 to 1990.

5 Synthesize ideas about the Berlin Wall.

6 Organize facts about the Soviet leaders during the Cold War.

7 Discover patterns of Soviet aggression during the Cold War.

8 List and organize facts about the Cuban Missile Crisis.

9 Create a graphic organizer illustrating the causes of the Cold war.

10 Describe the factors that contributed to the end of the Cold War.

Adventures Through World History! • Rickey Millwood
Kagan Publishing • 1 (800) 933-2667 • www.KaganOnline.com

Visual/Spatial

1 Watch the movie *The Missiles of October*.

2 Draw a frightening scene from the Cold War.

3 Create a collage of the famous leaders during the Cold War.

4 Create a PowerPoint about a major Cold War event.

5 Create a chart that displays the military strength of the NATO and Warsaw Pact.

6 Create a political cartoon about Nikita Khrushchev.

7 Create a visual display of the Soviet leaders during the Cold War.

8 Design a crossword puzzle using Cold War vocabulary terms.

9 Create a PowerPoint about Operation Crossroads.

10 Make a time line of the major events that occurred in the Soviet Union during the presidency of Mikhail Gorbachev.

11 Watch the film *The Day After*.

12 Create a political cartoon about the Soviet invasion of Afghanistan in 1979.

13 Watch *Miracle on Ice*.

Musical/Rhythmic

1 Identify and listen to 10 songs about nuclear war.

2 Find 10 songs about peace during the Cold War.

3 Listen to the song "Eve of Destruction" by Barry McGuire.

4 Evaluate any music by the Beatles that advocates world peace.

5 Find any songs about Cold War events.

6 Listen to the antiwar songs of Peter, Paul, and Mary.

7 Write a rap song about a major Cold War leader.

8 Listen to the song by Charlie Daniels called "In America."

9 Write a song about the Berlin Wall.

10 Identify and evaluate the protest music of the 1960s that relates to the Cold War.

11 Listen to any songs about nuclear war by Bob Dylan.

12 Listen to the song "Give Peace a Chance" by John Lennon

Adventures Through World History! • Rickey Millwood
Kagan Publishing • 1 (800) 933-2667 • www.KaganOnline.com

Chapter 16 continued
The Cold War
(1945–1991)

Bodily/Kinesthetic

1 Perform a skit about a family trying to escape from East Berlin as the wall is being constructed.

2 Build a model of the Berlin Wall.

3 Role-play the United Nations Security Council in an attempt to resolve the Cuban Missile Crisis.

4 Role-play an American and Russian family during the Cuban Missile Crisis.

5 Act out the role of a cosmonaut or astronaut during the Cold War.

6 Build a model of the Sputnik.

7 Act out the role of an American scientist working on the Strategic Defense Initiative.

8 Role-play a Russian military officer discussing the situation in Afghanistan after the Soviet invasion in 1979.

9 Re-create the famous chess tournament between Bobby Fischer and Boris Spassky.

10 Role-play American basketball players discussing the final minutes of a loss to the Soviet Union in the 1972 Olympics basketball game.

Naturalist

1 Observe pictures of the devastation in Europe after World War II.

2 Describe the regions of Cuba where the nuclear missiles were hidden in 1962.

3 Categorize the materials used to construct the Berlin Wall.

4 Watch a film showing how the first astronauts landed in the ocean after returning to Earth.

5 Observe nuclear submarines off the coast of Georgia and Florida.

6 List the characteristics of a nuclear missile silo.

7 Visit an abandoned nuclear fallout shelter.

8 Categorize the biological weapons produced during the Cold War by the Soviet Union and the United States.

9 Examine photographs of nuclear tests in the ocean during Operation Crossroads.

10 Observe film of the first moonwalk.

11 Learn about the causes of nuclear winter.

12 Record the immediate changes Earth and its population would face during nuclear winter.

13 Research how hydrogen bombs affect the atmosphere.

14 Conduct research about the harmful effects of radiation from nuclear fallout.

Interpersonal

1 Reach a consensus explaining why the United States and the Soviet Union never engaged in a nuclear confrontation during the Cold War.

2 Debate the issue of placing Soviet missiles on the island of Cuba.

3 Interview each other about the Truman Doctrine.

4 Discuss with a classmate why Josef Stalin refused to accept any assistance from the Marshall Plan.

5 Debate the possible actions America could have taken during the Berlin Blockade in 1948.

6 Practice compromising a solution to the nuclear arms race.

7 Do a team presentation about the 1956 Hungarian uprising.

8 Discuss with a classmate how détente led to the signing of the SALT agreement.

9 Discuss with a classmate the implications of the Brezhnev Doctrine.

10 Write a collaborative paper on the events that led to the end of the Cold War.

Intrapersonal

1 Prioritize the major foreign policy goals of the United States during the Cold War.

2 Form an action plan that would have prevented the Communist takeover of Eastern Europe after World War II.

3 Describe your feelings about the Berlin Blockade of 1948.

4 Write about the mood changes in Americans after the Russians launched Sputnik.

5 Relate the content of America's stand against the Communists to America's war against terrorism.

6 Weigh alternatives to a nuclear arms race during the Cold War.

7 Respond to the hypothetical situation of an all-out nuclear war between the United States and the Soviet Union.

8 Write a code of ethical conduct for the testing of nuclear weapons.

9 Choose between the alternatives of allowing missiles to remain in Cuba or destroying the missiles with air strikes.

10 Write about the tearing down of the Berlin Wall.

11 Write about the relationship of Mikhail Gorbachev and Ronald Reagan during the Cold War.

12 Weigh alternatives to building nuclear bomb shelters throughout America during the Cold War.

13 Write a personal poem about any Cold War event.

14 Describe your feelings about life as an American during the Cold War.

16.1 Blackline Master • Intrapersonal Activity

The Cold War

The Berlin Wall

In 1961, the Berlin Wall was constructed of concrete and barbwire to separate East and West Berlin. Each day thousands of people poured into West Berlin from Eastern Europe in search of freedom. To the Communists, this was quite embarrassing. If Communism was the perfect form of government, why were thousands fleeing each day? Nikita Khruschev, the premier of the Soviet Union, decided to erect a barricade through Berlin to seal off the two sections of the city. The penalty for trying to escape to West Berlin was death. The Berlin Wall was one of the most recognizable and hated symbols of the Cold War. It came crashing down in 1989 as the Cold War reached its conclusion.

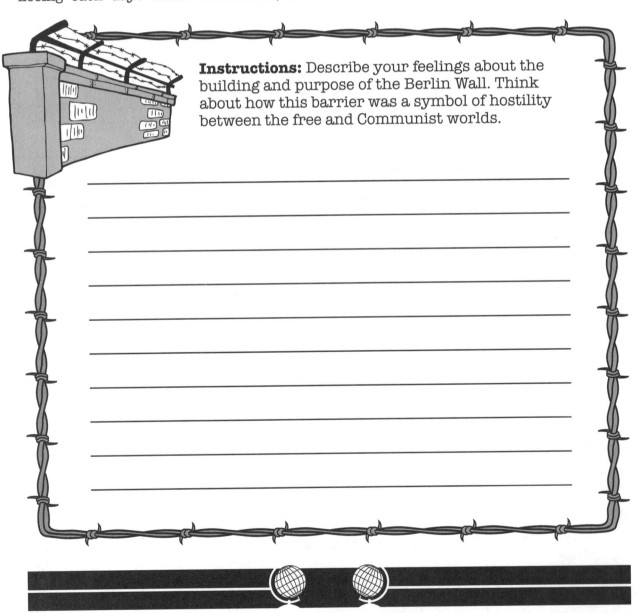

Instructions: Describe your feelings about the building and purpose of the Berlin Wall. Think about how this barrier was a symbol of hostility between the free and Communist worlds.

_____
_____
_____
_____
_____
_____
_____
_____
_____
_____

Adventures Through World History! • Rickey Millwood
Kagan Publishing • 1 (800) 933-2667 • www.KaganOnline.com

The Cold War

Nuclear Showdown over Cuba

The Cuban Missile Crisis was one of the most terrifying moments of the entire Cold War. In 1959, Fidel Castro became the dictator of Cuba. America and Cuba severed diplomatic ties and Castro became closely aligned with the Soviet Union.

In 1962, the United States discovered over 40 Soviet nuclear missiles on the island of Cuba. The missiles were placed there by Premier Nikita Khruschev. These weapons were capable of killing half of America's population in minutes.

President Kennedy forced the Russians to back down and remove the missiles. For a week in October 1962, the world was at the brink of a nuclear war between the Soviet Union and the United States.

Instructions: President Kennedy has asked your team to prepare the U.S. course of action during the Cuban Missile Crisis. Discuss your ideas as a team and write a summary.

16.3 Blackline Master • Logical/Mathematical Activity

The Cold War

The Soviet Invasion of Afghanistan

On Christmas Day 1979, the Soviet Union launched an offensive into Afghanistan. There was a world outcry to this imperialistic move. The United States regarded this invasion as an attempt by the Soviet Union to spread Communism and move closer to the Persian Gulf region. The 1980 Olympics were in Moscow but many nations—including the United States—boycotted the games.

The Soviet Union remained in Afghanistan for 10 years. The United States assisted the resistance fighters by shipping arms to Pakistan. Osama bin Laden led guerrilla fighters in Afghanistan against the Soviets. This adventure cost the Soviet Union a large amount of money and lives. President Mikhail Gorbachev decided to end the invasion in 1989.

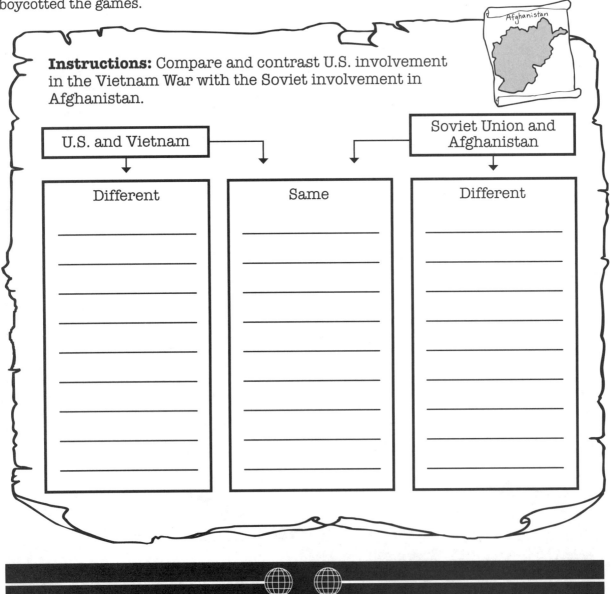

Instructions: Compare and contrast U.S. involvement in the Vietnam War with the Soviet involvement in Afghanistan.

U.S. and Vietnam | Soviet Union and Afghanistan

Different | Same | Different

16.4 Blackline Master • Visual/Spatial Activity

 # The Cold War

The Theory of Nuclear Winter

During the 1980s, a theory came out that stated an all-out nuclear war might result in what would be called *nuclear winter*. According to some of the world's leading scientists, the planet would first rapidly cool down. This would lead to catastrophic results for the planet and any humans who survived the original explosions.

How many nuclear explosions would it take to cause a nuclear winter? That answer is unknown. Some scientists believe that the survivors of a nuclear war would face a planet contaminated with radiation.

What percentage of Earth's population would survive an all-out nuclear war? Any survivors would face food shortages, disease, and famine. In reality, no winner would emerge in a nuclear war.

Instructions: Create a scene showing the effects of nuclear winter on Earth.

Adventures Through World History! • Rickey Millwood
Kagan Publishing • 1 (800) 933-2667 • www.KaganOnline.com

Chapter 17: Events in Asia after World War II

(1945–1995)

The nations of China, India, and Japan underwent drastic changes after the conclusion of World War II. Japan was transformed into a democracy and is today a leading world economic power. China was transformed into a Communist nation under Chairman Mao and is a developing nation with tremendous potential. India was finally given its independence from Britain after many years of struggle. China, India, and Japan were all important players during the Cold War years. The United States and the Soviet Union were aware of the economic and military importance of these three Asian nations.

Verbal/Linguistic

1 Share ideas about the American occupation of Japan after World War II.

2 Write a newspaper article about the economic conditions in Japan immediately after World War II.

3 Share ideas about Mahatma Gandhi and his nonviolent movement in India.

4 Do a descriptive writing exercise about the caste system in India.

5 Do a creative writing exercise about the dismissal of General Douglas MacArthur during the Korean Conflict.

6 Analyze the goals of the Green Revolution in India.

7 Discuss how Chairman Mao was able to establish a Communist government in mainland China in 1949.

8 Compare and contrast Mao's Great Leap Forward with Stalin's Five-Year Plans.

9 Explain America's policy of containment in Asia.

10 Write newspaper articles about North Korea's invasion of South Korea in 1950.

Logical/Mathematical

1 Compare and contrast India's independence with America's independence movement against Britain.

2 Evaluate the nonviolent resistance philosophy of Mahatma Gandhi.

3 Sequence the major events in the creation of India as an independent nation.

4 List and organize facts about East Pakistan.

5 Brainstorm ideas about Mao's Great Leap Forward.

6 Use inductive reasoning to explain why the Great Leap Forward was a calamity.

7 Create a graph illustrating the economic growth of China from 1949 to today.

8 Predict the combined population of China and India by the year 2050.

9 Discover trends in the policies of Communist dictators in Asia.

10 Determine the cost of American lives in the Korean Conflict.

Adventures Through World History! • Rickey Millwood
Kagan Publishing • 1 (800) 933-2667 • www.KaganOnline.com

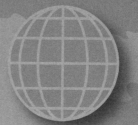

Visual/Spatial

1 Draw a scene about Japan immediately following World War II.

2 Watch the film *Gandhi*.

3 Create a political cartoon about Chiang Kai-shek and Mao Tse-tung.

4 Create a scene about the Great Leap Forward in China.

5 Examine scenes of life on Chinese communes.

6 Watch a film of President Nixon's visit to the People's Republic of China.

7 Create a cartoon about Ping Pong Diplomacy.

8 Draw a scene about India and Pakistan's nuclear programs.

9 Design a postcard about the Korean Conflict.

10 Create a PowerPoint about the Korean Conflict.

11 Observe pictures of the Korean memorial.

12 Draw a cartoon of America's decision to protect Taiwan from the People's Republic of China.

13 Examine the national flags of India, China, North Korea and South Korea.

14 Find and examine a picture of President Nixon visiting the Great Wall of China.

Musical/Rhythmic

1 Listen to the Chinese National anthem: "March of the Volunteers."

2 Interpret the lyrical meaning of the "March of the Volunteers."

3 Write a poem about the Great Leap Forward.

4 Listen to a Chinese military band honoring President Nixon upon his arrival to China.

5 Create a song about Richard Nixon's visit to China.

6 Listen to a national song of India, "Vande Mataram."

7 Create a song about Mahatma Gandhi and his nonviolent movement.

8 Compare and contrast American musical instruments of the 1950s with the musical instruments from China and India.

9 Listen to the national anthem of Japan, "Kimigayo."

10 Report on a famous Japanese, Chinese, or Indian musician.

Adventures Through World History! • Rickey Millwood
Kagan Publishing • 1 (800) 933-2667 • www.KaganOnline.com

Chapter 17 continued
Events in Asia after World War II (1945–1995)

Bodily/Kinesthetic

1 Act out the role of Mahatma Gandhi in leading a nonviolent protest in India.

2 Build a model of a famous structure in India or China.

3 Perform a pantomime about the Communist takeover of China in 1949.

4 Perform a skit about the Cultural Revolution in China.

5 Act out the role of President Nixon on his historical journey through China.

6 Role-play the United Nations as the People's Republic becomes the official government of China.

7 Interview a soldier that fought in the Korean Conflict.

8 Visit the Korean Memorial.

9 Plan an event to honor the soldiers that fought in the Korean Conflict.

10 Perform a skit about President Carter granting full diplomatic recognition to the People's Republic of China.

11 Create a display of items made in China.

12 Visit China or search the Internet and report to the class on your observations of that nation.

Naturalist

1 Categorize the materials used to make the clothing worn by Mahatma Gandhi.

2 Examine photographs of Gandhi's Salt March to the sea.

3 Record the changes in agricultural practices in India after receiving its independence from Britain.

4 List the goals of the Green Revolution in India.

5 Make a list of the natural resources found in Manchuria.

6 Describe the layout of a commune in the People's Republic of China.

7 Build a model of the Great Wall of China.

8 Record the developmental stages in China's Great Leap Forward.

9 Examine pictures on the Internet of Taiwan.

10 Observe the mountainous terrain of Korea.

11 Learn about the climate of Korea that Americans soldiers faced in the Korean Conflict.

12 Explain why the Hindus consider the Ganges River to be a sacred or holy river.

13 Examine photographs of China's Three Gorges Dam.

14 Examine pictures of the bridges that connect all four of Japan's major islands.

Adventures Through World History! • Rickey Millwood

Interpersonal

1 Do a team presentation illustrating how life in Japan changed after World War II.

2 Discuss with a classmate the role that the United States played in changing Japan after World War II.

3 Interview a classmate about Chairman Mao Tse-tung.

4 Do a team presentation on the relationship between the United States and the People's Republic of China in 1950.

5 Share with others your thoughts about American intervention in the Korean Conflict.

6 Do group presentations about current women's rights in Japan, China, North Korea, South Korea, and India.

7 Debate the American foreign policy of containment.

8 Discuss the relationship between the Soviet Union and China during the Cold War years.

9 Discuss the influence of President Nixon's visit to China.

10 Discuss with a classmate the obstacles India faced in its drive toward independence.

11 Share ideas about China's Four Modernizations.

12 Share with classmates the major ecological concerns in China, India, and Japan.

13 Discuss America's current relationship with Taiwan.

14 Discuss how Jawaharlal Nehru's family worked to modernize the state of India.

Intrapersonal

1 Describe your feelings about a nonviolent approach to India's independence after World War II.

2 Prioritize the needs of the population of India in the 1950s.

3 Meditate on the causes of conflict between the Hindus and Moslems in India after independence came.

4 Weigh alternatives to the Nationalist Chinese fleeing to Taiwan.

5 Express your likes and dislikes about the commune system set up by Chairman Mao.

6 Take a stance for America's involvement in the Korean Conflict.

7 Respond to the hypothetical situation of America using nuclear weapons in the Korean Conflict.

8 List the top priorities of Chairman Mao once he was firmly in power in China.

9 Write a personal poem about the recovery of Japan from nuclear destruction.

10 Defend the position by the United Nations to admit the People's Republic of China into the United Nations and oust Nationalist China (now known as Taiwan).

11 Think about how your life would be today if you lived in the People's Republic of China.

17.1 Blackline Master • Interpersonal Activity

Events in Asia after World War II

India's Struggle for Independence

The nation of India struggled to gain its independence from Britain through the 1930s and 1940s. Britain was determined to hold on to India as part of the British Empire and control the entire economy of India. Every aspect of life in India was dominated by the British.

The Indian Independence Movement was led by Mahatma Gandhi. He took a nonviolent approach. Indian independence was achieved through nonviolent measures such as protests, marches, strikes, and boycotts. The resistance broke the will of the British. Finally, in 1947, independence came as Gandhi predicted.

Instructions: Write 10 questions you would ask Gandhi. When done, ask a partner one of your questions. He/she must respond in the role of Gandhi. Then respond to your partner's question in the role of Gandhi. Find a new partner for each question.

1. _____
2. _____
3. _____
4. _____
5. _____
6. _____
7. _____
8. _____
9. _____
10. _____

Adventures Through World History! • Rickey Millwood
Kagan Publishing • 1 (800) 933-2667 • www.KaganOnline.com

17.2 Blackline Master • Verbal/Linguistic Activity

Events in Asia after World War II

The Recovery of Japan

Germany and Japan were both devastated after World War II. The United States took on the responsibility of economically and politically rebuilding these nations. The United States recognized an opportunity to assist these nations in recovery and convert former enemies into close allies. Today, these nations are leading world economic powers and are two of America's closet allies.

Instructions: Compare and contrast the military occupation, political restructuring, and economic rebuilding of Germany and Japan after World War II.

Germany	Japan
Military Occupation	
Political Restructuring	
Economic Rebuilding	

Events in Asia after World War II

The People's Republic of China

China became a Communist nation in 1949 as Chairman Mao came to power. This was terrible news for the United States because mainland China had been lost to a political ideology that opposes democracy. The Nationalists had to flee mainland China to Formosa (now called Taiwan). Formosa, often threatened by Mao, was guarded by the American navy.

Chairman Mao was determined to build up China's industry and agriculture quickly through the 1950s and 60s. He began a program called the Great Leap Forward and wanted to be seen as the leader of the Communist world.

This program was an economic disaster because it created giant communes that failed and small factories that could not produce quality goods. Work was regimented and families were torn apart. Mao ignored ideas from the West and his nation suffered a traumatic period of chaos.

Instructions: Describe five reasons the Great Leap Forward has been called a disaster.

17.4 Blackline Master • Naturalist Activity

Events in Asia after World War II

The Korean Conflict

In June 1950, North Korea launched a major offensive against South Korea in an attempt to unify the nation. The North was determined to establish a Communist dictatorship over the peninsula. North Korea had the backing of both the Soviet Union and China. The United States quickly rushed to the assistance of South Korea. This action was an example of America's containment policy. The goal was to stop the aggression of Communism.

For the next three years, war raged on the peninsula. Chinese soldiers entered the fray, and eventually the conflict ended in a stalemate. South Korea remained free but was constantly threatened. The United States and North Korea are on bitter terms today. North Korea has produced several nuclear weapons and long-range missiles, which the United States perceives as a major threat to world peace.

Instructions: Write a hypothesis about how the physical characteristics of Korea made the war extremely difficult for American soldiers in 1950. Use the outline to formulate your beliefs.

Hypothesis: _____
_____

I. Rugged Mountains
A. _____
B. _____
C. _____

II. Ocean Tides
A. _____
B. _____
C. _____

III. Heavy Snow
A. _____
B. _____
C. _____

IV. Extreme Cold
A. _____
B. _____
C. _____

V. Monsoons
A. _____
B. _____
C. _____

Adventures Through World History! • Rickey Millwood
Kagan Publishing • 1 (800) 933-2667 • www.KaganOnline.com

Chapter 18: Turmoil in Southeast Asia (1945–2000)

Indochina was in total chaos for much of the last half of the 20th century. War raged in Vietnam, refugees streamed out of Laos, and the Khmer Rouge came to power in Cambodia. The Khmer Rouge committed atrocities in Cambodia on a scale that the world had not seen since the Holocaust. The United States became involved in this region as a result of the domino theory and the policy of containment. North Vietnam launched an attack on South Vietnam; the United States responded with a long-term commitment in Vietnam. The United States left the region in 1973, and South Vietnam was immediately conquered by the North. Today, the entire region suffers from poverty, overpopulation and the AIDS epidemic.

Verbal/Linguistic

1. Explain the determination of France to control Vietnam after World War II.
2. Share ideas about Ho Chi Minh.
3. Read about the importance of the battle of Dien Bien Phu.
4. Write a summary of the Geneva Accords.
5. Write a speech explaining how and why America became involved in Vietnam.
6. Explain the concept of containment and the domino theory.
7. Do a descriptive writing exercise about the Viet Cong, including the tunnel network.
8. Write a newspaper story about the Gulf of Tonkin incident.
9. Read about the Khmer Rouge in Cambodia.
10. Discuss the policy of genocide in Cambodia under Pol Pot.
11. Read about Vietnam's invasion of Cambodia.
12. Read about recent outbreaks of avian bird flu in Southeast Asia.

Logical/Mathematical

1. Compare and contrast French and American involvement in Vietnam.
2. Brainstorm ideas about the goals of Ho Chi Minh in Vietnam.
3. Make a graph illustrating the cost of French involvement in Vietnam from 1945 until 1954.
4. Discover trends in America's involvement in Asian affairs after World War II.
5. Sequence the events that led to America's involvement in Vietnam.
6. Create a chart illustrating the American loss of life in Vietnam from 1961 until 1973.
7. Organize facts about the Khmer Rouge in Cambodia.
8. Compare and contrast the policies of Adolf Hitler and Pol Pot.
9. Make a graph illustrating the number of refugees that fled Laos and Cambodia from 1975 until 1985.

Adventures Through World History! • Rickey Millwood
Kagan Publishing • 1 (800) 933-2667 • www.KaganOnline.com

Visual/Spatial

1 Examine political cartoons of America's involvement in Vietnam.

2 Draw a scene about the Gulf of Tonkin incident.

3 Chart the route of the Ho Chi Minh Trails.

4 Estimate the distance across Vietnam that was sprayed with Agent Orange by the United States.

5 Create a scene of the effects of Agent Orange in Vietnam.

6 Create a graphic organizer that displays the strategy of the United States in Vietnam.

7 Examine famous pictures and scenes about the Vietnam Conflict.

8 Create a PowerPoint about the Vietnam Conflict.

9 Imagine you were an 18-year-old American being sent to the jungles of Vietnam in 1968.

10 Create a crossword puzzle about the major events in Southeast Asia after World War II.

11 Design a series of postage stamps about the Vietnam Conflict.

12 Watch the film *The Green Berets*.

13 Watch the film *No Time for Tears*.

14 Examine pictures of the Vietnam Memorial.

15 Examine scenes of the boat people that fled the Khmer Rouge of Cambodia.

Musical/Rhythmic

1 Listen to the music of Jimi Hendrix.

2 Listen to the song "Ballad of the Green Berets" by Barry Sadler.

3 Listen to the song "Ball of Confusion" by the Temptations.

4 Listen to the song "Eve of Destruction" by Barry McGuire.

5 Listen to the song "War" by Edwin Starr.

6 Listen to the song "I Feel Like I'm Fixin' to Die" by Country Joe McDonald.

7 Learn about the musical instruments played in Southeast Asia.

8 Compose a melody of songs about the Vietnam Conflict.

9 Compare and contrast the music from World War II with the music of the Vietnam Conflict.

10 Evaluate the protest music of the 1960s and determine the impact it had on the Vietnam Conflict.

11 Sing songs before the class about the Vietnam Conflict.

12 Interpret the lyrical meaning to the song "Fortunate Son" by Creedence Clearwater Revival.

Chapter 18 continued
Turmoil in Southeast Asia
(1945–2000)

Bodily/Kinesthetic

1 Act out the role of a French soldier after the fall of Dien Bien Phu.

2 Role-play an American sailor talking about the Gulf of Tonkin incident.

3 Perform a skit about Hanoi Hanna.

4 Role-play an America POW from the Vietnam Conflict.

5 Interview an American that served in the Vietnam Conflict.

6 Build a model of the Hanoi Hilton.

7 Conduct research about the use of napalm and Agent Orange in Vietnam.

8 Visit the Vietnam Memorial.

9 Act out the role of a Viet Cong discussing the tunnel complexes.

10 Write a play about a tour of duty in Vietnam.

11 Act out the role of a young American that has just been conscripted into the Army.

12 Act out the role of a hippie or antiwar protestor.

13 Interview someone that remembers the Kent State Massacre.

14 Re-create the trial of William Calley after the My Lai Massacre.

15 Interview a refugee that escaped the Khmer Rouge of Cambodia.

Naturalist

1 List the characteristics of the topography of the nations on the Indochina Peninsula.

2 Classify the vegetation found in Vietnam.

3 Examine pictures of the Ho Chi Minh Trails.

4 Classify the different types of agents sprayed on the jungles of Vietnam.

5 Record the significance of the Gulf of Tonkin incident.

6 Categorize the natural materials the Viet Cong used to make booby traps.

7 Watch a film that shows the tunnel network that concealed the Viet Cong.

8 Identify any deadly species of snakes found in Vietnam.

9 Examine pictures of rice paddies in Southeast Asia.

10 Create a display of the major foods consumed in Southeast Asia.

11 List the characteristics of the boats used to carry refugees from Cambodia to Thailand.

12 Classify the types of insects that annoyed American soldiers in Vietnam.

Interpersonal

1 Interview a person that served in the Vietnam Conflict.

2 Invite a Vietnam Conflict veteran to speak to the class.

3 Make a team project about America's involvement in Vietnam.

4 Debate the issue of using napalm and Agent Orange in Vietnam.

5 Discuss with a classmate the impact of the Gulf of Tonkin incident.

6 Make a team project about anti-Vietnam War songs.

7 Watch a movie about Vietnam, and then discuss its historical accuracy.

8 Read, then discuss a novel about the Vietnam Conflict.

9 Plan an event to honor those that served in the Vietnam Conflict.

10 Interview a person that left Southeast Asia after the United States abandoned the region in 1975.

11 Reach a consensus on why the Vietnam Conflict turned sour for the United States.

12 Discuss as a class the reasons explaining why America failed to prevent a communist takeover of South Vietnam.

13 Practice taking turns criticizing the actions of Presidents Johnson and Nixon over decisions made in Vietnam.

14 Debate the American decision to abandon Vietnam in 1973.

15 Discuss with a classmate the gruesome goals of the Khmer Rouge and their ruthless leader Pol Pot.

Intrapersonal

1 Think about the goals of Ho Chi Minh after World War II.

2 Write about the decision by France to leave Vietnam in 1954.

3 Defend the decision by President Kennedy to send American soldiers to the aid of South Vietnam.

4 Describe your feelings about the military draft.

5 Observe the mood changes in Americans after the Gulf of Tonkin incident.

6 Write about the needs of a young American soldier in Vietnam.

7 Write a personal poem about American women who served in Vietnam.

8 Describe your feelings about the treatment of American POWS in the Hanoi Hilton.

9 Express your likes or dislikes about President Nixon's decision to leave Vietnam in 1973.

10 Write a personal poem about the use of Agent Orange in Vietnam.

11 Relate America's involvement in Vietnam to America's involvement in Iraq.

12 Make an action plan that the United Nations could have implemented to have prevented the murder of millions in Cambodia by the Khmer Rouge.

13 Write a story as if you were one of the boat people escaping Cambodia and the Khmer Rouge.

18.1 Blackline Master • Intrapersonal Activity

Turmoil in Southeast Asia

American's Excursion into Vietnam

America's long and costly excursion in Vietnam still causes haunting memories today. Over 58,000 Americans died in the jungles of Vietnam to stop the spread of Communism. America sent military advisors to Vietnam in the early 1960s but by 1966, nearly three hundred thousand soldiers were in Vietnam. The buildup continued and over one half million Americans were in Vietnam by the late 1960s.

The war took a dramatic turn for the worse in 1968 when the North Vietnamese launched the TET Offensive. After this event, Richard Nixon was elected president and he promised to end the conflict. Five years later, America finally left Vietnam.

This would be the first war in American history that we did not win. Were the reasons justified for involving we in this war? Was Vietnam essential to America's security?

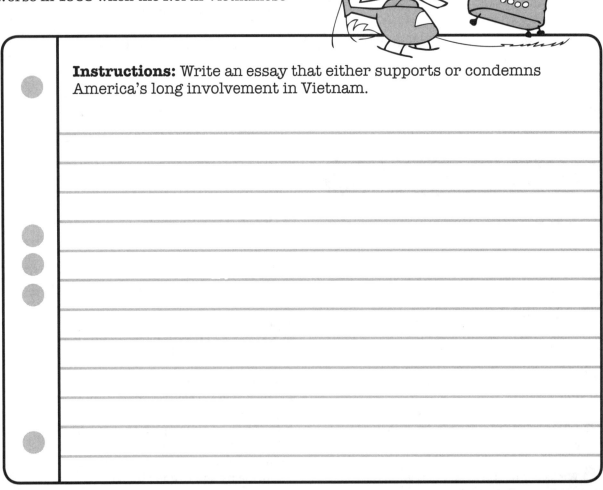

Instructions: Write an essay that either supports or condemns America's long involvement in Vietnam.

Turmoil in Southeast Asia

The Tunnels Hid the Cong

The Viet Cong or South Vietnamese traitors who assisted the North Vietnamese were clever and used guerrilla warfare in their fight against the United States. America was totally unprepared to engage in this type of warfare. The Viet Cong, often referred to as Charlie, intended to send as many Americans as possible home in body bags. Their mission was to frustrate and drag out the war until Americans turned against the conflict.

The Viet Cong received the supplies from the North down a series of jungle roads called the Ho Chi Minh Trails. These trails ran through Laos and Cambodia.

The Viet Cong soldiers often lived under the ground in a network of tunnels. They stayed there in the day and came out to attack Americans at night. These tunnels often contained booby traps. Small American soldiers called tunnel rats were forced to go into these tunnels in search of the enemy. These nightmarish assignments were extremely dangerous. Today, these tunnels are open for tourists to visit.

Instructions: Create a drawing that depicts the network of tunnels that hid the Viet Cong.

18.3 Blackline Master • Musical/Rhythmic Activity

Turmoil in Southeast Asia

Patriotic and Antiwar Music

The Vietnam Conflict produced a flood of protest music. These songs were heard on the radio every hour, and as the situation worsened in Vietnam, the protest songs increased. The songs played a role in influencing public opinion about the war in Vietnam.

There were a few patriotic songs such as "The Ballad of the Green Beret," but by the end of the conflict, these songs were seldom heard. Most of the singers of these antiwar songs were young people because it was their generation that was being devoured by this drawn-out war. Protest songs, such as WAR by Edwin Starr, sent a powerful message.

Instructions: Identify and listen to 10 songs about the Vietnam War. Select one song and explain how you feel this song affected the people that heard it on the radio or in a concert. Remember to listen to both patriotic and antiwar songs.

1. _____
2. _____
3. _____
4. _____
5. _____
6. _____
7. _____
8. _____
9. _____
10. _____

_____
_____
_____

Adventures Through World History! • Rickey Millwood

Turmoil in Southeast Asia

Genocide in Cambodia

After the United States left Indochina, a Communist group called the Khmer Rouge came to power in Cambodia. They changed the name of the country to Kampuchea and began a policy of genocide to de-westernize the nation. Led by Pol Pot, the Khmer Rouge killed a million of its own people. Professionals and those that spoke English were some of the first slaughtered with picks and axes.

The world had not witnessed such ruthless killing since the Holocaust. Refugees fled the nation by the thousands while the rest of the world watched and did virtually nothing to help the people of this nation. This gruesome scene was made into a very powerful and emotionally stirring movie known as *The Killing Fields*.

Instructions: Do a descriptive writing exercise about the Khmer Rouge and their leader Pol Pot. Be sure to include the changes the Khmer Rouge made to establish their new nation of Kampuchea.

Chapter 19: Recent Events in the Middle East (1975–2007)

America and the world's economy depend heavily on the Middle East because it contains 60% of Earth's petroleum. However, the region is torn by war and acts of terrorism, and is one of the most volatile places on the globe. In 2001, Osama bin Laden orchestrated the terrorist attack on the United States. This provoked the United States to remove the Taliban from power in Afghanistan and launch an attack on Iraq. As of 2007, U.S. troops remain in Iraq despite public opinion opposed to the war.

Verbal/Linguistic

1. Write about the significance of the Camp David Accords.

2. Write a biography of Anwar Sadat, Osama bin Laden, or Saddam Hussein.

3. Discuss America's historical relationship with Israel.

4. Discuss America's differing relationship with Iran before and after 1979.

5. Do a descriptive writing exercise about the Iranian Revolution in 1979.

6. Compare and contrast Ayatollah Khomeini with Saddam Hussein.

7. Debate the implications of the Russian invasion of Afghanistan in 1979.

8. Write a poem about the OPEC cartel.

9. Read about the use of chemical weapons in the war between Iran and Iraq during the 1980s.

10. Write a research report on the Iraqi invasion of Kuwait and Desert Storm.

11. Write a newspaper article about the events on 9-11-01.

12. Write a report about America's invasion of Iraq in 2003.

Logical/Mathematical

1. Sequence the major events that led to the Camp David Accords.

2. Analyze data about oil reserves in the nations of the Middle East.

3. Make a graph illustrating the number of barrels of petroleum that are exported from the Persian Gulf region annually.

4. List and organize facts about the Suez Canal.

5. Make associations between Israel and the United States.

6. Determine the number of deaths in the Iran-Iraqi War.

7. Graph the rise of oil per barrel price from 2002–2007.

8. Estimate the price of gasoline per gallon by 2015.

9. Compare and contrast Hamas and Hezbollah.

10. Brainstorm ideas explaining how Osama bin Laden might have been captured after 9-11-01.

11. Draft a plan to bring peace to the Middle East.

Adventures Through World History! • Rickey Millwood

Visual/Spatial

1 Create a political cartoon that reflects the power of OPEC.

2 Watch the film *Not Without My Daughter*.

3 Create a scene about the record high gasoline profits the oil companies are making.

4 Design a map that illustrates the current trouble areas in the Middle East.

5 Create a political cartoon about Iran's nuclear capability.

6 Design a monument to honor the victims of 9-11-01.

7 Imagine you were a reporter covering America's invasion of Iraq in 2003.

8 Make a poster about the Taliban in Afghanistan.

9 Design a wanted poster for Osama bin Laden.

10 Create a PowerPoint depicting the treatment of women in Afghanistan while the Taliban were in power.

11 Imagine being Lebanese and caught in the crossfire between Hezbollah and Israel.

12 Create a graphic organizer illustrating America's war against terrorism beginning with 9-11-01.

13 Imagine how life has changed in America since 9-11-01.

Musical/Rhythmic

1 Listen to the Israeli national anthem "Hatikva."

2 Listen to Egypt's national anthem "Bilady, Bilady, Bilady."

3 Analyze why Egypt's national anthem was rewritten in 1979.

4 Listen to Charlie Daniel's "In America" played during the Carter administration.

5 Listen to Lee Greenwood's "God Bless the USA"—a popular song during Desert Storm.

6 Listen to John Michael Montgomery's "Letters From Home."

7 Listen to Alan Jackson's "Where Were You When the World Stopped Turning"—a song about 9-11-01.

8 Write a rap song about the current war in Iraq.

9 Write a rap song about the high price of gasoline.

10 Write a song about the hunt for Osama bin Laden.

11 Write a poem about world terrorism.

12 Learn about current music that is popular in the Arab world.

13 Compare and contrast the current music heard about the conflict in Iraq with music heard during the Vietnam era.

14 Write a patriotic song about America's stand for democracy around the globe.

Adventures Through World History! • Rickey Millwood
Kagan Publishing • 1 (800) 933-2667 • www.KaganOnline.com

Chapter 19 continued
Recent Events in the Middle East (1975–2007)

🌐 Bodily/Kinesthetic

1 Build a model of an oil derrick.

2 Interview a soldier who served in Desert Storm.

3 Role-play the soldiers who captured Saddam Hussein.

4 Role-play American citizens who witnessed the attack on the World Trade Centers in 2001.

5 In groups, discuss the best policy to protect America from terrorist attacks.

6 Role-play Israeli citizens who were attacked by Hezbollah rockets.

7 Role-play Lebanese citizens discussing the bombing of their nation by Israel in the summer of 2006.

8 Act out the role of the OPEC nations as they discuss current oil production.

9 Perform a skit about the high price of gasoline.

10 Perform a pantomime about executives from major oil companies and enormous profits from gasoline sales.

11 Complain about recent gasoline prices without talking.

12 Explore information about new hybrid cars.

🌐 Naturalist

1 Record information about the Suez Canal.

2 List the major features of the Persian Gulf.

3 Examine pictures of the Sinai Peninsula.

4 Observe photos of oil fields through Saudi Arabia.

5 Examine pictures of ecological damage to Kuwait by Saddam Hussein.

6 Observe the changes to the Persian Gulf after it was polluted with oil by Saddam Hussein during Desert Storm.

7 Record the vital importance of the Strait of Hormuz.

8 Examine pictures of manmade islands off the coast of the United Arab Emirates.

9 Examine the beach resorts of Dubai.

10 Determine how beach resorts in the Persian Gulf affect marine wildlife.

Interpersonal

1 Discuss with a classmate the reasons Iran and Iraq were at war through the 1980s.

2 Do a team presentation on the political goals of Hamas and Hezbollah.

3 Share with others facts about America's current involvement in Iraq.

4 Do a team presentation on Iran's nuclear program.

5 Practice taking turns naming the nations most friendly and those most hostile to the United States.

6 Reach a consensus explaining why President Reagan launched an air strike against Libya in 1986.

7 Interview classmates about Iraq's invasion of Kuwait.

8 Do a team presentation on important characters in the Middle East.

9 Solve problems that Americans confront against insurgents in Afghanistan and Iraq.

10 Practice constructive criticism of America's involvement in the Middle East.

11 Mediate an end to the conflict between Hezbollah and Israel.

Intrapersonal

1 Defend the position by the United States to fully support Israel in the Middle East.

2 Make an action plan that would conclude or expand America's involvement in Iraq.

3 Take a stance for America's involvement in Afghanistan.

4 List the top priorities of the United States in the Middle East.

5 Write about the capture and trial of Saddam Hussein.

6 Observe American spending habits due to the high price of gasoline.

7 Think about the actions the United Nations should take against Iran's nuclear program.

8 Weigh alternatives to the dependency on oil from the Middle East.

9 Defend the position of Israel to invade Lebanon.

10 Write about the needs of the Lebanese citizens as a result of the war between Israel and Hezbollah.

11 Form an action plan that you would have implemented to capture Osama bin Laden.

19.1 Blackline Master • Intrapersonal Activity

Recent Events in the Middle East

Crisis in Iran

Iran, a nation that was once one of America's closet allies in the Middle East, now poses a threat to world security. The Iranian Revolution in 1979 shattered the friendship with the United States. The Shah fled Iran only to be replaced by Ayatollah Khomeini. President Carter allowed the Shah to reside in the United States as he was dying with cancer. However, the Ayatollah demanded his return for execution. President Carter refused to return the Shah to Iran and the Iranian revolutionaries then seized the U.S. embassy and held American embassy workers captive for 444 days.

The relationship between the United States and Iran was never mended. Iran's partnership with North Korea is of greatest concern to the United States since North Korea has produced both nuclear weapons and long-range missiles.

Instructions: Write about the actions you feel the United States should take toward Iran's determination to develop nuclear weapons and acquire long-range missiles from North Korea.

Adventures Through World History! • Rickey Millwood
Kagan Publishing • 1 (800) 933-2667 • www.KaganOnline.com

19.2 Blackline Master • Visual/Spatial Activity

Recent Events in the Middle East

Insurgency in Iraq

In the early 1990s, the United States fought a war against Iraq to remove Iraqi forces from the small nation of Kuwait. This was accomplished through Operation Desert Storm. Saddam Hussein, the Butcher of Baghdad, remained in power under the close watch of the United Nations.

In 2001, the United States was attacked by terrorists and Osama bin Laden. The United States responded by removing the Taliban from power in Afghanistan and then launched an attack on Iraq in 2003.

President George W. Bush firmly believed that Saddam Hussein harbored weapons of mass destruction and was determined to remove him from power. The president believed the ousting of Saddam Hussein would prevent more terrorist attacks against the United States. The Iraqi people would then be free from this ruthless dictator. Saddam was captured by American soldiers, but insurgents who supported him are causing a massive wave of violence all over Iraq.

In January 2007, President Bush announced his plan to send an additional 21,500 American soldiers to Iraq. The newly elected Democratic Congress and President Bush differ on the issue of a further troop buildup in Iraq.

Perhaps the words of Lieutenant Colonel Andrew Myers sum up the feelings of so many American soldiers in Iraq. When asked about his mission in Iraq against the insurgency, Lieutenant Myers replied, "My mission is to help the Iraqi counterparts develop the operational, logistical, and administrative capabilities to defeat their opponents then return to my family."

Instructions: Create a political cartoon about America's current involvement in Iraq.

Adventures Through World History! • Rickey Millwood
Kagan Publishing • 1 (800) 933-2667 • www.KaganOnline.com

19.3 Blackline Master • Verbal/Linguistic Activity

Recent Events in the Middle East

The Struggle Against Al-Qaeda

American soldiers face extremely dangerous conditions in Iraq each day. The country is filled with supporters of Saddam Hussein and terrorist members of Al-Qaeda. These forces of Al-Qaeda, which moved into Iraq, were led by Al Zarqawi. The United States learned of his location and eliminated him with a bombing raid. Terrorist attacks continue in Iraq against American soldiers.

Suicide bombers and roadside bombs are causing most of the deaths and severe injuries. Despite a large American military presence and billions of dollars being spent in Iraq, the objective of establishing a democracy and lasting peace in Iraq is a slow process. Americans tend to believe that the United States will be involved in Iraq for many years to come.

Instructions: Write a letter as if you were an American soldier currently stationed in Iraq facing daily attacks from insurgents. Write your letter to a family member or friend and describe the current situation in Iraq.

Adventures Through World History! • Rickey Millwood
Kagan Publishing • 1 (800) 933-2667 • www.KaganOnline.com

19.4 Blackline Master • Logical/Mathematical Activity

Recent Events in the Middle East

The Price of Oil

In 1974, OPEC nations placed an oil embargo against the United States due to America's support of Israel. This action showed just how dependent Americans were on foreign sources of crude oil. During the 1980s and 90s the price of oil fell as Iraq and Iran were in a bitter war. These two oil producers were cutting the price of oil to quickly move more of the commodity in order to purchase more weapons.

In the spring and summer of 2007, the price of gasoline soared on a daily basis. There was much more competition around the world for oil—and that demand drives up the price. Oil hit an all-time high with prices climbing to over $80 per barrel. That pushed gasoline to nearly $4 per gallon in the United States.

Instructions: Make two graphs illustrating the price of oil per barrel and gasoline per gallon in 1967, 1977, 1987, 1997, and 2007. Explain why the prices fluctuate.

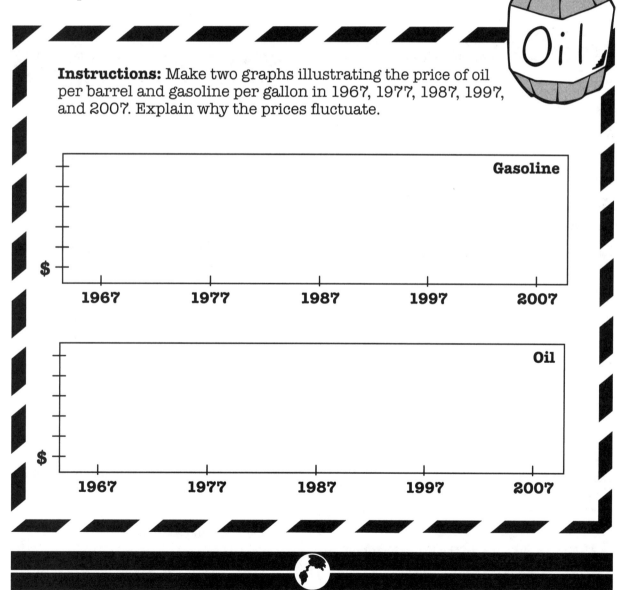

Adventures Through World History! • Rickey Millwood
Kagan Publishing • 1 (800) 933-2667 • www.KaganOnline.com

Chapter 20: Recent Events in the Modern World (1980–2007)

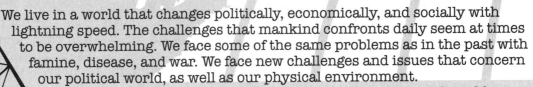

We live in a world that changes politically, economically, and socially with lightning speed. The challenges that mankind confronts daily seem at times to be overwhelming. We face some of the same problems as in the past with famine, disease, and war. We face new challenges and issues that concern our political world, as well as our physical environment.

The end of the Cold War gave a glimmer of hope toward world peace, but recent acts of terrorism around the globe disrupt any thoughts of a peaceful planet. Yet, as members of the human race, we strive to solve problems to make our world a better place to live.

Verbal/Linguistic

1 Read about Mikhail Gorbachev and the breakup of the Soviet Union.

2 Explain the concept Glasnost.

3 Share ideas about the fall of Communism in Eastern Europe.

4 Write about the Tiananmen Square Massacre in China.

5 Share ideas about apartheid in South Africa.

6 Write a biography of Nelson Mandela.

7 Write a research paper about AIDS in African nations.

8 Do a descriptive writing exercise about the end of the Cold War.

9 Write a report on weapons of mass destruction.

10 Write a poem about child labor around the world.

11 Create a newspaper article on a major environmental issue the world faces.

12 Write a proposal to the United Nations to create peace in Iraq.

Logical/Mathematical

1 Brainstorm ideas that led to the end of the Cold War.

2 Sequence the major events in the breakup of the Soviet Union.

3 Organize facts about democratic revolutions in Eastern Europe.

4 Compare and contrast life today in Western and Eastern Europe.

5 Discover patterns in world terrorism.

6 Make a graph showing the expansion of the world's population from 1985 until today.

7 Make predictions about the spread of AIDS over the next decade.

8 List facts about the causes of recent famines in Africa.

9 Sequence the events in South Africa that led to the end of apartheid.

10 Make predictions about America's dependency on petroleum.

11 Synthesize ideas that would bring peace between Israel and Hezbollah.

Visual/Spatial

1 Create a political cartoon about the breakup of the Soviet Union.

2 Create a political cartoon about the fall of the Berlin Wall.

3 Create a drawing about the effects of global warming.

4 Draw a scene about apartheid in South Africa.

5 Make a PowerPoint about 9-11-01.

6 Create a chart about avian influenza.

7 Create a graphic organizer about five current world problems.

8 Design a picture of the automobile of the future.

9 Design buildings that can withstand major earthquakes.

10 Make a PowerPoint about the Indonesian tsunami.

11 Create a postcard to promote world peace.

12 Make a clay sculpture of a famous modern-day athlete.

13 Make a PowerPoint about the modern Olympics.

14 Make a PowerPoint about the uses of nuclear energy.

15 Visualize major changes in the world over the next century.

Musical/Rhythmic

1 Listen to the song "We Are the World."

2 Listen to the song "Free Nelson Mandela."

3 Evaluate the effect that music has had on recent historical events.

4 Write a song about a current world event.

5 Listen to John Lennon's "Give Peace a Chance."

6 Evaluate the impact that American music has around the world.

7 Listen to songs calling attention to AIDS.

8 Listen to current patriotic music about America's involvement in Iraq.

9 Identify entertainers who have gone to Iraq to entertain American soldiers.

10 Compose a melody about an environmental issue.

11 Create a song about equality for women around the world.

Chapter 20 continued
Recent Events in the Modern World (1980–2007)

Bodily/Kinesthetic

1 Act out the role of a witness to the Tiananmen Square Massacre in Beijing.

2 Role-play an eyewitness to the destruction of the Berlin Wall.

3 Perform a skit about the end of the Cold War.

4 Role-play women from various nations speaking about equal rights.

5 Role-play South Africans speaking about the system of apartheid.

6 Re-create a fascinating moment from the 2004 Olympics.

7 Conduct a science experiment related to global warming.

8 Draw pictures of medical instruments of the future.

9 Act out the role of an American soldier who has just returned from Afghanistan or Iraq.

10 Design a computer game about a recent event in history.

Naturalist

1 Record the changes in Earth's temperature over the last 100 years.

2 List the characteristics of acid rain.

3 Examine photographs of the tsunami that devastated Indonesia.

4 List the characteristics of Hurricane Katrina.

5 Record the changes in Louisiana and Mississippi due to Hurricane Katrina.

6 Examine photographs of the destruction of Lebanon due to the fighting between Israel and Hezbollah.

7 Record the changes in the Amazon rain forest since 1990.

8 Create a graphic organizer illustrating the causes of an environmental issue.

9 Examine a piece of the Berlin Wall in a museum.

10 Conduct research about the avian bird influenza.

11 Conduct research about the West Nile virus.

12 List the characteristics of desertification.

13 Research laws on the pollution of oceans.

14 Make a chart of the nations with nuclear weapons.

Interpersonal

1 Do a team presentation on the fall of the Soviet Union.

2 Discuss with a classmate the breakup of Communism across Eastern Europe.

3 Share with others information about the Tiananmen Square Massacre.

4 Plan an event honoring the victims of 9-11-01.

5 Discuss the reasons for America's involvement in Iraq.

6 Practice taking turns stating how America can combat terrorism.

7 Write a collaborative report an on environmental issue.

8 Mediate an end to the hostility between Israel and Hezbollah.

9 Practice taking turns criticizing America's involvement in a current world hotspot.

10 Share with other classmates information about the recent civil war in Rwanda.

11 Do a class presentation on ethnic cleansing in the Balkans.

12 In pairs, discuss how North Korea poses a threat to world peace.

13 Make a team project about a current world problem.

Intrapersonal

1 Describe your feelings about America's involvement in Iraq.

2 Observe the mood changes in America after 9-11-01.

3 Form an action plan that would end famine across Africa.

4 Form an action plan that would prevent North Korea from selling nuclear weapons.

5 Meditate on the greatest problems the world will face in the next decade.

6 Express your likes and dislikes about America's war on terrorism.

7 Take a stance to defend Israel's attack on Hezbollah.

8 Weigh alternatives to the war between Israel and Hezbollah.

9 Form an action plan to educate the world's citizens about AIDS.

10 Write a personal poem about an event in modern history.

11 List the top priorities of the world's leading environmentalists.

12 Write about what you feel should be the top priorities of the United Nations.

13 Defend the position by the United States to promote democracy around the world.

14 Write about the wants and needs of human beings.

15 Write your personal thoughts about what the United Nations should do about Iran's nuclear production.

Adventures Through World History!

Political Events and Issues

20.1 Blackline Master • Visual/Spatial Activity

Recent Events in the Modern World

The Tiananmen Square Incident

In 1989, a major uprising took place in the People's Republic of China. Thousands of Chinese students gathered in Tiananmen Square in Beijing. These students were protesting Communism and the mismanagement of government. Many of these were Chinese students who had lived and studied in the United States and desired change for China.

Soviet President Mikhail Gorbachev was in Beijing for a visit. When he departed, the Chinese authorities launched an all-out military offensive on these students. Several thousand students were shot and bayoneted. Some were crushed by army tanks.

Americans in China captured much of the incident on video. The world was horrified by the incident. The Chinese authorities left no doubt that they were still in complete control of the nation. The Chinese government has denied there was an uprising and say that no massacre ever occurred.

Instructions: Draw a scene about the Tiananmen Square Massacre.

Adventures Through World History! • Rickey Millwood
Kagan Publishing • 1 (800) 933-2667 • www.KaganOnline.com

Political Events and Issues

20.2 Blackline Master • Verbal/Linguistic Activity

 # Recent Events in the Modern World

Apartheid in South Africa

South Africa, one of the most important African nations on the continent, was shunned by most of the world over its policy of apartheid. Even though South Africa is rich in gold and diamonds, most of the people are very poor. The term *apartheid* means apartness; the people in South Africa were separated by race. The majority of people were once brutally ruled by a white minority—those who protested apartheid were murdered or jailed.

The most famous person imprisoned who resisted apartheid was Nelson Mandela. With the end of apartheid, in the early 1990s, he was released and later became president of South Africa. Today, South Africa has rejoined the family of nations.

Instructions: Read about the Sharpeville and Soweto massacres in South Africa. Then, write a story as if you were a newspaper reporter covering one of the scenes.

NEWS

Adventures Through World History! • Rickey Millwood
Kagan Publishing • 1 (800) 933-2667 • www.KaganOnline.com

Political Events and Issues

20.3 Blackline Master • Interpersonal Activity

Recent Events in the Modern World

The Fall of the Soviet Union

One of the most riveting moments in history occurred in 1991 when the Soviet Union collapsed. This Communist nation had been forged by the dictators Lenin and Stalin. This nation had helped defeat Nazi Germany in World War II but became America's opponent for more than 40 years during the Cold War.

Most Western political analysts did not predict this collapse. The Soviet Union had placed most of its budget into defense spending; this drained the nation's economy. The military spending to support the Warsaw Pact nations was another constant strain on the nation. In addition, the Soviet Union had supported and propped up Communist dictators all over the world. In 1979, the Soviet Union began a 10-year war in Afghanistan that further strained the nation's economy.

During the mid-1980s, an energetic man named Mikhail Gorbachev became the president of the Soviet Union. He attempted to reform the nation with his policy of openness and gave his people more freedoms than they had experienced in decades. He attempted to restructure the nation's economy, but his policies failed. The nation was not prepared for drastic economic reforms because everything in the nation had been rigidly controlled by the government.

Parts of the Soviet Union began to break away. The Baltic States were the first to declare independence. Gorbachev declined to use force—and the nation transformed into independent states. Mikhail Gorbachev was the last president of the Soviet Union.

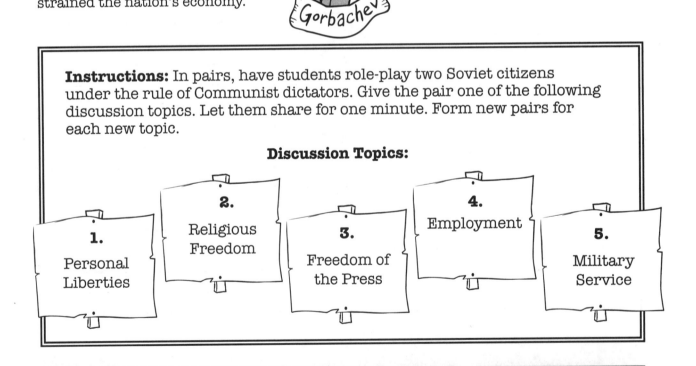

Instructions: In pairs, have students role-play two Soviet citizens under the rule of Communist dictators. Give the pair one of the following discussion topics. Let them share for one minute. Form new pairs for each new topic.

Discussion Topics:

1. Personal Liberties
2. Religious Freedom
3. Freedom of the Press
4. Employment
5. Military Service

Recent Events in the Modern World

Ethnic Cleansing in the Balkans

Yugoslavia was ruled by President Josip Broz, better known as Tito, until his death in 1980. Yugoslavia was the only nation in Eastern Europe that had its own brand of Communism and was not under the rule of the Soviet Union. Tito was a strong ruler; his personality and tactics held the nation together until his death.

Serious trouble began in 1991 when Slovenia and Croatia announced they were leaving the nation of Yugoslavia to become independent states. The nation began to fragment. Several major ethnic groups in the former Yugoslavia began to vie for power. The major groups included the Croats, Serbs, and Muslims.

Some of the groups did not want their new nations split into regions based on ethnicity. Bitter fighting erupted in Bosnia as the Serbs began a policy of massive killing of the Muslims; this became known as "ethnic cleansing." The Serbs were attempting to remove Muslims from the regions they desired to control.

The Serbian forces in Bosnia were backed by Serb leader Slobodan Milosevic. More than 200,000 people died in the former Yugoslavia through the 1990s. Crimes against humanity were also committed by the Muslims and Croats. However, Milosevic was viewed as the main perpetrator of these crimes.

Milosevic died in March 2006 while in prison. He was on trial charged with genocide and crimes against humanity. The atrocities committed in this region were on a scale similar to those seen in World War II.

Instructions: Write an article condemning the United Nations for allowing atrocities to be committed for several years in Bosnia before intervening came.

Political Events and Issues

20.5 Blackline Master • Interpersonal Activity

 # Recent Events in the Modern World

Civil War in Rwanda

During the 1980s, a bitter civil war erupted in the African nation of Rwanda. This conflict involved the Hutu and Tutsi tribes, and the atrocities that followed shocked the world. Perhaps a million people died before the genocide ended.

With the end of the Cold War, many African nations that supported either the United States or the Soviet Union were totally abandoned. In 1994, all-out fighting erupted between these groups in Rwanda. The United Nations was slow to react, and the world witnessed slayings that were unbelievable. President Bill Clinton has stated that this is the one foreign policy issue he failed to respond to adequately before the situation was completely chaotic.

Instructions: In pairs, form a plan that the United Nations should have employed to prevent the genocide in Rwanda.

Political Events and Issues

20.6 Blackline Master • Musical/Rhythmic Activity

Recent Events in the Modern World

World Terrorism

There was a brief glimmer of hope for peace after the Cold War, but terrorism continues to threaten life daily around the globe. Terrorists threaten to use, and attempt to gain access to, weapons of mass destruction that were once only held by the superpowers. These weapons include biological, chemical, and nuclear materials.

Diseases that scientists have fought to eradicate in the past are now being made into weapons. Smallpox is perhaps the most frightening of all these deadly germs. This disease has claimed more lives than any other disease.

Instructions: Listen to the song "Eve of Destruction" by Barry McGuire. Write about how the lyrics of song apply to the world today.

Adventures Through World History! • Rickey Millwood

Political Events and Issues

20.7 Blackline Master • Logical/Mathematical Activities

Recent Events in the Modern World

Fighting in Southern Lebanon

In July 2006, Hezbollah launched a barrage of missiles from Lebanon into Israel. Thousands of missiles were fired into Israeli towns daily. Israelis in Haifa were terrorized by these Katyusha and Fajr rockets.

It appears that Iran and Syria are most responsible for aiding Hezbollah. Israel responded with a massive bombing campaign against Lebanon and even launched a limited invasion with its army to wipe out Hezbollah strongholds. As usual, ordinary citizens have suffered and have had to evacuate from southern Lebanon.

Activity Options

1. List and organize facts about Hezbollah and the Katyusha rockets.

2. Make predictions about the future of Lebanon.

Adventures Through World History! • Rickey Millwood
Kagan Publishing • 1 (800) 933-2667 • www.KaganOnline.com

Recent Events in the Modern World

The Beginning of Conflict with Iraq

The United States and Iraq fought in early 1991 in Operation Desert Storm. The Americans drove Iraq out of Kuwait after the forces of Saddam Hussein had invaded that small nation. Saddam claimed that Kuwait was a part of Iraq and that Kuwait was stealing Iraq's oil with illegal drilling under Iraq's border. Neither of these accusations were true, but Saddam intended to take over Kuwait's oil fields.

The United States crushed Saddam's army in a matter of weeks. Before leaving Kuwait, Saddam ordered his Republican Guard units to torch the oil fields of Kuwait. It took months for the U.S. forces to extinguish hundreds of colossal fires. Saddam also ordered for oil pipes to be opened to flood the Persian Gulf with petroleum. These were both acts of ecological vandalism.

Instructions: Write a personal memoir as if you were an American soldier that witnessed the damage to Kuwait and the Persian Gulf by the Republican Guard of Iraq.

Dear _____,

Political Events and Issues

20.9 Blackline Master • Logical/Mathematical Activity

Recent Events in the Modern World

Saddam Hussein's Execution

On December 30th, 2006, Saddam Hussein, known as the "Butcher of Baghdad," was executed. Saddam had been placed on trial by the Iraqi government and was found guilty of crimes against humanity, which included the mass murder of 148 Shiitite Muslims and the death of 180,000 Kurds. The United States turned him over to the Iraqi authorities for execution, and the death sentence was carried out in swift fashion.

Saddam's trial was filmed and a verbal exchange took place between Saddam and his executioners in the last minutes of his life. Saddam was hanged, and his body was taken back near his home town of Tikrit.

The future of Iraq is very much in doubt. Americans view the war differently with each passing day. The situation in Iraq has turned out much differently than Americans anticipated. Some groups want America to begin to withdraw from Iraq immediately while others call for an increased buildup.

An increasing percentage of Americans now see America's role in Iraq as a policeman between the Sunni and Shiitie Muslims, rather than a war against terrorism. The cost in lives and dollars grows daily. Over 3,000 Americans have now died in Iraq, and the insurgency movement continues.

Instructions: Predict what the future holds for Iraq now that Saddam has been executed. Share your predictions with a partner.

1-year outlook _____

_____

_____

_____

5-year outlook _____

_____

_____

_____

20-year outlook _____

_____

_____

_____

Adventures Through World History! • Rickey Millwood
Kagan Publishing • 1 (800) 933-2667 • www.KaganOnline.com

Political Events and Issues

20.10 Blackline Master • Interpersonal Activities

Recent Events in the Modern World

The United Nations

The United Nations (UN) was created after World War II to promote world peace and harmony among nations. This organization faces a wide variety of problems. The UN deals with political, social, legal, and economic issues. Which problems or situations today do you feel need immediate discussion by the United Nations?

Imagine being an ambassador in the United Nations from a country other than the United States. How do you feel that would affect your decision to examine world problems in a different light? If we view a world crisis through the eyes of another nation, how could that give us a deeper knowledge of the problem and insight toward the best solution?

Activity Options

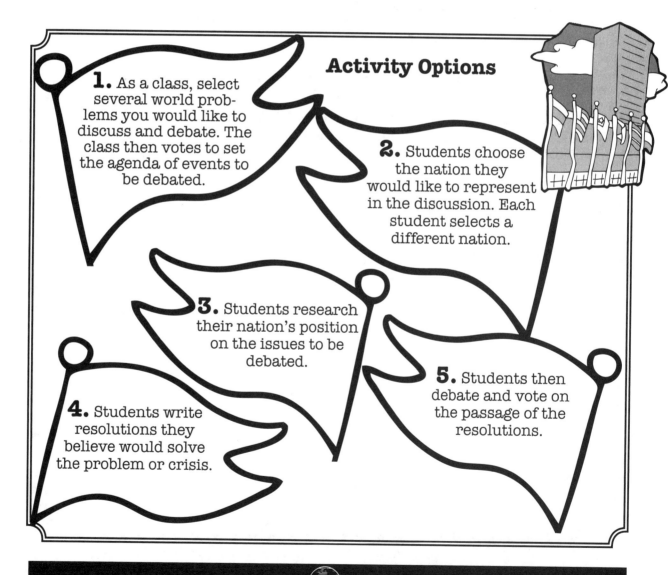

1. As a class, select several world problems you would like to discuss and debate. The class then votes to set the agenda of events to be debated.

2. Students choose the nation they would like to represent in the discussion. Each student selects a different nation.

3. Students research their nation's position on the issues to be debated.

4. Students write resolutions they believe would solve the problem or crisis.

5. Students then debate and vote on the passage of the resolutions.

Adventures Through World History! • Rickey Millwood
Kagan Publishing • 1 (800) 933-2667 • www.KaganOnline.com

Political Events and Issues

20.11 Blackline Master • Visual/Spatial Activity

Recent Events in the Modern World

Nuclear Proliferation

The United States was the first nation in the world to develop and use atomic weapons. After World War II, the Soviet Union, France, and Britain also produced atomic weapons. By the 1950s, atomic bombs were replaced with even more powerful weapons called hydrogen bombs.

Nations produced nuclear weapons and new delivery systems capable of sending nuclear weapons anywhere in the world in a matter of minutes. Some estimates indicated that perhaps as many as 50,000 nuclear weapons existed during the height of the Cold War.

Today, many nations have nuclear weapons. North Korea has developed and tested a nuclear device; Iran is involved in nuclear research and production. Iraq is no longer capable of producing a nuclear weapon with the elimination of Saddam Hussein. However, there is great concern that nuclear weapons produced by North Korea or Iran could end up in the hands of terrorists.

Instructions: Create a political cartoon illustrating how the United States should approach the nuclear programs of North Korea and Iran.

Environmental Issues

20.12 Blackline Master • Bodily/Kinesthetic Activity

Recent Events in the Modern World

Industrial Accidents

Two of the worst industrial accidents in world history occurred during the 1980s. The first took place at the Union Carbide pesticide plant in Bhopal, India. This accidental release of toxic gases caused the instant death of nearly 10,000 people. Thousands more suffered severe lung problems and have continued to perish over the decades that have followed. Today, the death count stands at more than 25,000.

Another industrial accident occurred at the Chernobyl nuclear facility in the Ukraine. This accident has been blamed on improperly trained workers and a faulty reactor. The facility released nuclear material, which covered much of the area of Belarus. Scientists predict that up to 4,000 people could die as a result of exposure to this radiation.

Instructions: Research, then act out one of the following scenarios in response to an industrial accident.

- Union Carbide public relations specialist in a press interview regarding the Bhopal disaster

- Chernobyl nuclear facility employee

- Wife of a Bhopal victim

- CEO of Union Carbide

- Soviet Union government official

Adventures Through World History! • **Rickey Millwood**
Kagan Publishing • 1 (800) 933-2667 • www.KaganOnline.com

Environmental Issues

20.13 Blackline Master • Naturalist Activity

 # Recent Events in the Modern World

Global Warming

The theory of global warming states that over the last century, Earth's temperature has risen. It warns that if this continues, there will be a further melting of polar ice caps and a rise in ocean levels. One of the main causes of global warming is the burning and emission of fossil fuels.

Supporters of this theory attribute the rash of violent hurricanes to global warming. Hurricanes feed off warm water. As the ocean temperatures rise, the magnitude of hurricanes increase. Opponents of global warming believe that weather patterns occur over long spans of time. They feel that there is not enough data to support the claim that global warming is causing recent category five hurricanes.

Evidence, however, does support that Earth's temperature has risen over the last century. In February 2007, the Intergovernmental Panel on Climate Change released a 20-page report on global warming. Evidence collected by hundreds of scientists indicates that the planet is warming; they feel this is "very likely" caused by mankind.

Instructions: List the characteristics of global warming and record the environmental changes associated with this phenomena.

Characteristics
_____
_____
_____
_____
_____
_____
_____
_____
_____
_____
_____
_____
_____

Environmental Changes
_____
_____
_____
_____
_____
_____
_____
_____
_____
_____
_____
_____
_____

Adventures Through World History! • Rickey Millwood
Kagan Publishing • 1 (800) 933-2667 • www.KaganOnline.com

Environmental Issues

20.14 **Blackline Master • Interpersonal Activity**

Recent Events in the Modern World

Acid Rain

Today, acid rain is a major environmental issue around the world. This problem first started in Europe as a result of the Industrial Revolution.

Acid rain is caused by the burning of coal and the release of pollutants into the atmosphere. This usually occurs at electricity plants as sulfur dioxide is released into the atmosphere. This mixes in the clouds and falls back to Earth in rain or snow.

Acid rain can have a devastating effect on forests. Today, forests are completely bare as a result of acid rain. Acid rain also falls into lakes and rivers. This has an extremely harmful effect on the aquatic life in the marine chain. Fish cannot live in water that contains a low pH.

Acid rain is a problem that humans will continue to confront in the future. Our surroundings are so fragile and delicate; we must make every attempt to preserve the environment in its natural state.

Instructions: In groups of four, do team presentations about acid rain. Consider the following factors in your presentations.

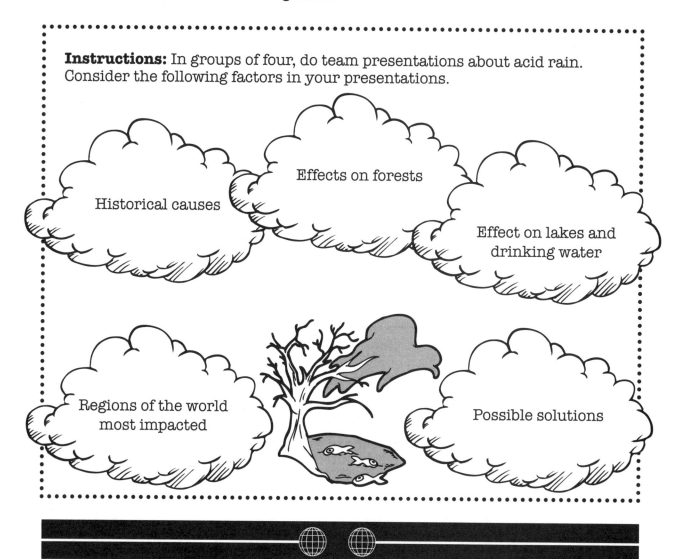

- Historical causes
- Effects on forests
- Effect on lakes and drinking water
- Regions of the world most impacted
- Possible solutions

Adventures Through World History! • Rickey Millwood
Kagan Publishing • 1 (800) 933-2667 • www.KaganOnline.com

Environmental Issues

20.15 Blackline Master • Intrapersonal Activity

Recent Events in the Modern World

Deforestation of the Amazon

Photos from the space shuttle clearly show that large areas of the Amazon rain forest have been devastated. This massive cutting of timber in the Amazon region affects both plant and animal life. The region is being cleared to make room for grazing land and soy bean production.

There has been a dramatic increase in the cutting of the Amazon rain forest over the last four years. A world out-cry during the 1990s slowed cutting, but the demand for the soy bean has once again intensified logging. The Amazon is fragile and contains almost half of the world's rain forest. This forest is vital because it helps provide the oxygen we breathe.

Instructions: In an essay, describe your feelings about the cutting of the Amazon rain forest to grow agricultural products. Collect your ideas below.

Adventures Through World History! • Rickey Millwood
Kagan Publishing • 1 (800) 933-2667 • www.KaganOnline.com

Environmental Issues

20.16 Blackline Master • Verbal/Linguistic Activity

Recent Events in the Modern World

The Tsunami of 2004

On December 26, 2004, a major earthquake occurred off the western coast of Sumatra. The quake measured a 9.1 on the Richter scale. This intense quake is the second most powerful quake ever recorded. The underwater quake produced a series of tsunami waves that slammed into 11 Asian nations.

The people of these nations had very little warning. Gigantic waves, some reaching over 100 feet in height, battered the coasts. These waves moved at a speed of several hundred miles per hour, little time for escape. Some islands and villages were completely swallowed. The island of Sri Lanka, just south of India, was obliterated in just minutes.

Estimates now put the death toll at more than 230,000. Former Presidents George H. Bush and Bill Clinton toured areas devastated and were horrified. Many people view the 2004 tsunami as the worst natural disaster in history.

Instructions: Complete a creative writing exercise as if you survived the tsunami that devastated Sri Lanka on December 26, 2004.

Adventures Through World History! • Rickey Millwood
Kagan Publishing • 1 (800) 933-2667 • www.KaganOnline.com

177

Social & Economic Events

20.17 Blackline Master • Logical/Mathematical Activity

Recent Events in the Modern World

The Spread of AIDS

The spread of AIDS around the globe continues at an alarming rate. Most Americans are familiar with AIDS due to a nationwide education campaign. However, many people in third-world nations have never even heard of AIDS and are totally uneducated about this epidemic. Today, it is estimated that forty million people around the world are HIV positive. This disease has claimed more than twenty million victims since 1980.

The U.S. Center of Disease Control estimates that more than one million Americans are infected. This number constitutes epidemic proportions.

Instructions: Create a graph illustrating through numbers which Asian and African nations are most affected by AIDS.

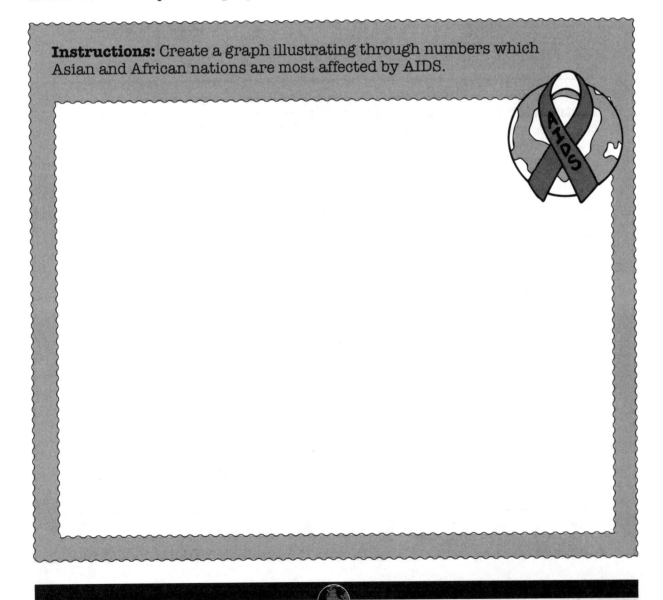

Social & Economic Events

20.18 Blackline Master • Naturalist Activity

Recent Events in the Modern World

Avian Bird Influenza

The Spanish flu, Hong Kong flu, and swine flu are three types of influenza that reached pandemic levels. Now, another strain of influenza is being closely watched by the world's leading epidemiologists—the avian bird influenza, or bird flu.

This disease is caused by a virus in the intestines of wild birds. The virus is transmitted to domestic birds through close contact. There is no vaccine to prevent this disease from being contracted by humans. Victims usually come into contact with infected birds such as ducks and chickens.

The strain of bird flu that physicians are most concerned with is H5N1. This disease causes great concern to the World Health Organization for several reasons. It results in high fever and muscle aches, and severely affects the respiratory system. Complications involving the lungs can often result in death.

Although the most common cases of the bird flu are in Asia and Africa, it appears the virus will continue to spread. There is a possibility that a pandemic could occur. In late January 2007, agricultural officials in South Korea destroyed 250,000 chickens contaminated with this deadly virus. As of 2007, approximately 160 people have died as a result of the bird flu.

Instructions: You are a top authority on the bird flu. Research and answer the following questions. Then take turns sharing your answers with a small group.

- ✔ What is the avian influenza?
- ✔ What countries have been affected?
- ✔ Is it safe to eat poultry?
- ✔ How do people become infected?
- ✔ How might this become a pandemic virus?
- ✔ What are warning signals that a pandemic is beginning?
- ✔ How can it be prevented/treated?
- ✔ Is the world prepared?

Adventures Through World History! • Rickey Millwood
Kagan Publishing • 1 (800) 933-2667 • www.KaganOnline.com

Social & Economic Events

20.19 Blackline Master • Bodily/Kinesthetic Activity

Recent Events in the Modern World

The Rising Cost of Gasoline

The world witnessed a dramatic increase in the rise of the cost of oil during 2006. The price of oil per barrel reached nearly $80. This drove up the price of gasoline to nearly $4 per gallon across America.

There are varying opinions as to why the price of oil escalated in such a short time. There is certainly more demand around the world for petroleum. However, oil companies are recording their highest profits ever. The high price of gasoline affects all segments of a nation's economy.

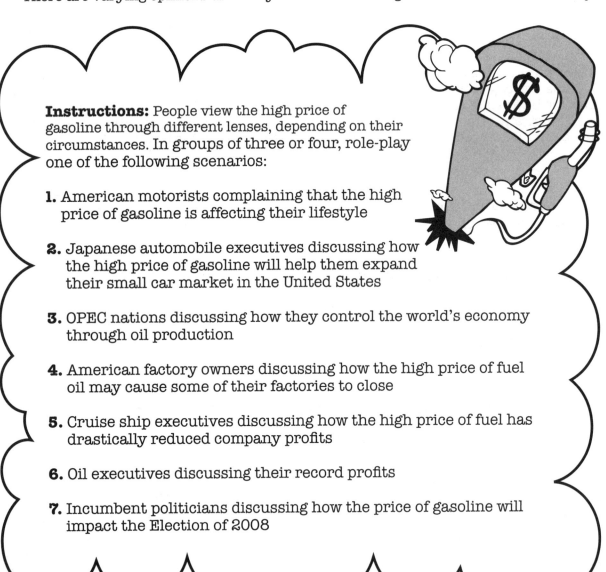

Instructions: People view the high price of gasoline through different lenses, depending on their circumstances. In groups of three or four, role-play one of the following scenarios:

1. American motorists complaining that the high price of gasoline is affecting their lifestyle

2. Japanese automobile executives discussing how the high price of gasoline will help them expand their small car market in the United States

3. OPEC nations discussing how they control the world's economy through oil production

4. American factory owners discussing how the high price of fuel oil may cause some of their factories to close

5. Cruise ship executives discussing how the high price of fuel has drastically reduced company profits

6. Oil executives discussing their record profits

7. Incumbent politicians discussing how the price of gasoline will impact the Election of 2008

Adventures Through World History! • Rickey Millwood
Kagan Publishing • 1 (800) 933-2667 • www.KaganOnline.com

Social & Economic Events

20.20 Blackline Master • Interpersonal Activity

Recent Events in the Modern World

Solving the Energy Crisis

All segments of industry are affected by high gasoline prices. New car and boat sales are dramatically down. Companies that use petroleum in their products are losing large amounts of money. The cost of food is up due to shipping; Americans are saving money by eating at home rather than at restaurants.

It appears that gasoline prices will continue to increase in the future. There is certainly more demand on the world market, especially by China and India. The recent increase in the price of gasoline has caused many families to restructure their budgets.

Instructions: In pairs, discuss the impact of the high price of gasoline. Then list possible saving tips for a family budget.

Adventures Through World History! • Rickey Millwood
Kagan Publishing • 1 (800) 933-2667 • www.KaganOnline.com

181

Social & Economic Events

20.21 Blackline Master • Visual/Spatial Activity

 # Recent Events in the Modern World

Trade Embargo Against Cuba

In 1959, Fidel Castro came to power on the island of Cuba. He announced he was a Communist and nationalized the industries in Cuba. He severed ties with the United States and began to trade with America's old political foe, the Soviet Union. Anti-Castro forces attempted to invade Cuba at the Bay of Pigs to oust Castro. This invasion failed as it lacked support from the United States.

In 1962, the Soviet Union placed nuclear missiles in Cuba and almost started a nuclear war with the United States. President John Kennedy led the United States through this tense crisis. War was avoided at the last moment when the Soviets dismantled and removed the missiles. Over the last 40 years, the United States has placed a trade embargo against Cuba in an attempt to choke the life out of Castro's nation. Americans are highly restricted from traveling to Cuba. Americans traveling abroad are not allowed to bring any products made in Cuba into the United States. Cuba, once an American vacation paradise, is still isolated by the United States. The thought that the Castro regime would fall as a result of end of the Soviet Union never materialized.

Instructions: Create an illustration demonstrating how the United States has attempted to strangle the economic life out of Cuba by a trade embargo.

Recent Events in the Modern World

World Famine

Each day thousands of children and adults die around the world because of famine. The continents of Africa and Asia are usually hardest hit. But some of the nations in the Western world also suffer from famine. Drought, war, insects, and crop failure from poor agricultural practices all contribute to this problem.

In the 1980s, Ethiopia suffered from a terrible famine. Singer Harry Belafonte suggested that musicians join together through their music to call attention to the desperate situation in Ethiopia. Lionel Ritchie and Michael Jackson wrote, "We Are the World," and the song was recorded by over 40 major singers in the United States. The song stayed number one for a month and raised millions of dollars for famine relief.

Instructions: Listen to the song "We Are the World." Recognize how it calls attention to world famine. Now compose your own song that would offer solutions to the problem of famine.

Social & Economic Events

20.23 Blackline Master • Intrapersonal Activity

 # Recent Events in the Modern World

A Changing World

The world we live in is forever changing. Today, we try to solve our problems with technology. However, sometimes technology brings on a host of problems we never imagined. For example, cell phones are very useful yet thousands of traffic fatalities occur each year in the United States as a result of people talking on these devices while driving. We are constantly attempting to make our lives easier, but sometimes we end up making them more complicated with technological changes.

Instructions: Write an essay describing your feelings about a recent invention that has been both beneficial and harmful to mankind.

Social & Economic Events

20.24 Blackline Master • Verbal/Linguistic Activity

Recent Events in the Modern World

Cloned Food Coming Soon

The Food and Drug Administrations has ruled that cloned food is safe to consume. This decision pleases some groups and angers others. Supporters believe that cloned animals will produce a higher quality of meat, milk, and eggs. Cloned food could be on the market as early as 2010.

As of 2007, there are less than 1,000 cloned animals in America. These animals will not be killed; they will be used for breeding stock. Cloned animals are expensive to produce—one animal can cost over $15,000.

Instructions: Conduct research about cloned animals. Then, write an essay supporting or condemning the FDA decision to allow cloned food on the market. Record your hypothesis and ideas below.

We Are Clones

 # Notes

 # Notes

 # Notes

 # Notes

 # Notes

Kagan
It's All About Engagement!

Kagan is the world leader **in creating active engagement in the classroom.** Learn how to engage your students and you will boost achievement, prevent discipline problems, and make learning more fun and meaningful. Come join Kagan for a workshop or call Kagan to **set up a workshop for your school or district**. Experience the power of a Kagan workshop. **Experience the engagement!**

SPECIALIZING IN:

- ★ Cooperative Learning
- ★ Win-Win Discipline
- ★ Brain-Friendly Teaching
- ★ Multiple Intelligences
- ★ Thinking Skills
- ★ Kagan Coaching

KAGAN PROFESSIONAL DEVELOPMENT

www.KaganOnline.com ★ 1(800) 266-7576

Kagan

It's All About Engagement!

Kagan is your source for active engagement in the classroom.

Check out Kagan's line of books, SmartCards, software, electronics, and hands-on learning resources—all designed to boost engagement in your classroom.

Books

SmartCards

Software

Learning Chips

Spinners

Learning Cubes

KAGAN PUBLISHING

www.KaganOnline.com ★ 1(800) 933-2667